DEAR KAMALA

RED ⚡ LIGHTNING BOOKS

COMPILED & EDITED BY **PEGGY BROOKS-BERTRAM**

DEAR KAMALA

WOMEN WRITE TO THE
NEW **VICE PRESIDENT**

This book is a publication of

Red Lightning Books

an imprint of
Indiana University Press
Office of Scholarly Publishing
Herman B Wells Library 350
1320 East 10th Street
Bloomington, Indiana 47405 USA

iupress.indiana.org

Manufactured in the United States of America

First printing 2021

Cataloging information is available from the Library of Congress.

ISBN 978-1-68435-162-6 (pbk.)
ISBN 978-1-68435-163-3 (web PDF)

CONTENTS

ACKNOWLEDGMENTS

I owe a special debt to Dr. Johnnetta Cole, President of the National Association of Black Women's Clubs who submitted a letter she wrote to Kamala Harris on behalf of the thirteen extraordinary Black Women's organizations of the National Association of Negro Business and Professional Women's Clubs, an organization representing more than 2,000,000 Black women around the world. That letter is published in this book. A special thanks to those women from Buffalo, New York, who believed in this project and responded rapidly to my requests for letters and shared their ideas with me. Thanks also to numerous women who tuned in from around the country to join hastily called Zoom meetings so that they could see other contributors and offer their comments about the project.

I thank my husband for his assistance and for his unending patience addressing my technology faults. A great thank-you to Jennifer Parker, the founder and owner of Jackson Parker Communications LLC, a public relations consulting firm that offers integrated marketing solutions, public relations, and community outreach. Jennifer walked me—on more than one occasion—through the bowels of social media, without which this work could not have been possible. She was indispensable for the web work, social media platform access, and her broad organizational skills. I am deeply indebted to her for her knowledge, support, and deep friendship and her "We Can Make it Work" mentality.

There were also numerous women who not only submitted their own letters but also notified their friends and colleagues about this project, urged them to submit a letter, and followed up on their submissions, letting no one fall through the cracks. I am especially indebted to Kadidia Doumbia from France, a specialist in gender education, for her assistance in identifying several women from the African continent; Diane Williams from Mississippi, who identified several poets and world-renowned celebrated storytellers and encouraged them to respond; and Arlette Miller Smith for referrals of other thoughtful writers. I am indebted to the expatriates such as Adrianne George from Sweden, who has worked within Democrats Abroad as the Global Caucus leader and Global Volunteers leader, as a member of the Global Black Caucus Steering Committee, and who is currently on the Affirmative Action Committee and is Sweden's Black Caucus Chair.

I owe a special thanks to all those women around the world who stopped in their tracks, wrote a letter, and called their friends, children, and other women and asked them to also write a letter to Kamala. And thanks to all of those women in different time zones who wrote letters and joined Zoom meetings and who woke up each morning to a loud, colorful fireworks video urging them to contribute. Deep thanks to all of them. And, thanks to all those women who gave me time and space on their blogs and podcasts, for example, Black Girl Nerds, Blavity.com, news stations and professionals such as Terry Wisdom with Harlem Network News, and myriad Facebook pages supporting Kamala Harris, such as When Black Women Gather, Black Women for Kamala Harris, Black Women in Suburbia, Black Women United for Kamala Harris, and many others.

It is important to acknowledge the Girl Scouts of America, particularly a group of young girls from California. The troop is led by Kristen Podulka, and when the young fifth graders indicated that they wanted to send letters to Kamala, Kristen dove right in and came back with twelve beautifully written and very thoughtful letters. These young girls are from myriad regions of the world including the US, India, and Australia. They are a beautiful addition to the *Dear Kamala* letters, and the topics they inquire about were myriad. They placed heavy emphasis on planet safety including clean oceans, cleaner air, and safety of animals in clean water. They asked Kamala to address major international issues such as the return of the United States to the Paris Agreement for climate change, and one expressed a desire to be a Supreme Court justice. They called for halting the spread of COVID 19, combating worldwide pollution, eliminating racism and discrimination in the country, and replacing plastic with compostable materials. All were concerned about global warming and the melting glaciers that affect the lives of the polar bears. Caring about current political divides, they asked the Vice President for her thoughts on how she thinks the country is currently being run. They called for decreased homelessness and expressed delight in seeing women of color be elected and called for legislation to enhance diversity and inclusion. That is a lot from a small group of fifth graders and it is powerful, and we thank them. These are tall orders for a new Vice President.

FOREWORD

The 30 Woman Company (1873)[1]

Something rotten was hangin over the suffocating air
that Friday afternoon when Ella, Janey, Lady Jones
and another 27 of us women decided to free Sethe from
[a] blood drenched past and [a] lunatic present. Walking dusty, determined and prepared, we brought ready
weapons—herbs, roots, Bibles and faith—to battle the
evil lurking at 124 Bluestone. We stopped shy of the
yard while . . . Mazey dropped to her knees and, like
tumbling dominoes, we all sank down into the dusty
brown earth—praying, mourning, whispering, sighing,
singing and praying the road down some mo':

Hear our prayer, oh Lord. Bring thy servant, Sethe, from the hovering
wickedness. Keep her strong, master. Put your
protective arms round 'bout her . . . Then cast
all evil back to hell. Fling it and cast it into the
sea of forgetfulness, Father. . . . Deliver Sethe
from her past sins . . . we ask you, Lord. Amen.
[But]

This is not a story
This is not a story to pass on;
This is not a story
This is not a story to pass on

This is a silentsufferingsong of a
wretchedwickedworld gone wrong
(Miller Smith).

In *Beloved*, Toni Morrison's iconic novel, a passel of determined women show up, speak up, and rise up in solidarity to save their estranged neighbor, Sethe, who was being terrorized by the past in her home at 124 Bluestone Road. Some of the women are reluctant participants in the rescue. They believe Sethe deliberately excluded them for 18 years from her misery; nevertheless, protecting their own outweighs her perceived arrogance and their lingering doubts.

One hundred and forty-seven years later, a woke company of willing womxn[2] stand up, buckle up, and write up their determination to *lift up*, not a Sethe haunted by the past, but a senator named Kamala Harris who was weaned from the womb—in the traditions of Sanskrit and Sankofa—to lead, to take back our country's present, unlock our future, bridge identity with heritage, salve pain and polarization, prosecute injustice and inequity: as the Vice President of these (un)United States.

In *Dear Kamala*, a compendium of greetings, advice, warnings, prayers, requests, affirmations, and demands spill onto pages addressed to Vice President Kamala Devi Harris. The letters, poems, and stories reflect the writers' individual voices, collective resolve, and strong belief that Kamala Harris's selection as the Vice President will ensure the restoration of justice, life, liberty, dignity, and fairness—for all. Well, if the truth really *be's* told, the writers' stance centers primarily on their own narratives of displacement and disillusionment. The womxn's[2] stories are designed to help Harris situate the rememory and continuation of America's pockmarked legacies (Bertram), especially racial enmity in education, housing, and employment. They call forth Harris as a strong, yet compassionate warriorwomxn capable of ameliorating our country's bitterness and near annihilation in 2020: the hurricanes, wildfires, and flooding; the squalid migrant detention camps; and the apocalyptic double pandemic of Covid-19 and racial upheaval. They also remind her that "she was born for this" new leadership role (Sandra) at a critical time and she must "welcome her destiny" (Celeste) that first grew in her amma's womb water. That Kamala must extract power, purpose, and perseverance from the intentionality of her name, lotus flower that grows thick, deep roots in muddy water; yet, the lotus rises above that murkiness—growing strength even through invading darkness, finally blooming with beauty, humility, knowledge, and power.

The time came. The writerwomxn gather their weapons—tea leaves, mother wit, fervent prayer, and righteous truth—then, in letters and poems and chants, each summons Kamala to claim her place at the next presidential table. They are confident she will win the vice-presidential seat but, if by chance, there is no designated *VP Harris* chair, she should remember: Shirley Chisholm left a folding chair for her from the "1972 Chisholm for President" campaign. And how difficult could it be for Harris to not only earn her seat at the table but also use her "I'm speaking" voice to halt any interference as she rightfully takes her seat. In fact, the writerwomxn muse across cyberspace: "she must carry her own seat with her by now. Look at how many times she's 'moved on up'—prosecutor. district attorney. Attorney General and Senator. They weren't ready then and sho' aint ready this time for an Asian, African American, Divine Nine, HBCU, Sistar VP married to a White lawyer cheerleader. Oh Yeah. She got her own chair."

> Calling all women, Calling all Sisters . . . First and second and third world women . . . Women in and outside the power structure . . . working women . . . welfare women . . . Questioning women . . . Ostracized. Tired of being penalized . . . Come help [Kamala] . . . bridge the gaps—Racial, cultural, or generation [al]. We want action and veneration.
> These men, these men they just ain't doing it.
> . . . had hundreds of years, Now they 'bout to ruin it . . .
> Old and young and middle-aged women. Now is the time for an evolution. Let's all search and [help] find a solution . . . .
> Oh yes. [And bring your letter].[3]

When SistaDoc Peggy Brooks-Bertram sent out the call for womxn to letter Kamala Devi Harris's path to *her* cabinet seat at the Head (of State) Table in the People's House, some—like the 30 Woman Company before—held their peace, cleared their throats, but then decided to support pass their doubt, while insisting that, once confirmed, Kamala strongly remind others and herself to do "the least amount of harm to those—already being harmed the most" (Lillian).

Sit. Sip. Savor, as you read the record of revolution by 100 womxn from Brooklyn to Buffalo to Baltimore and beyond who turned off their phones; packed up their lunches; kissed their lovers bye-bye; turned on waiting computers; and sat down in their truth writing notes of encouragement, support, and relief from their Black, Brown, Yellow, Red, and White Baby Boomer, Gen X, Y, and Z—English, French, Canadian, Nepalese, African speaking ebony, cocoa, saffron, coral, alabaster selves to the heart and head of the bloomed lotus flower called Kamala.

Arlette Miller Smith, PhD
African American Studies–English Department, retired 2020!
St. John Fisher College
Rochester, New York

Notes

1. The action in Toni Morrison's *Beloved* takes place between 1850 and 1873. In the book, the monologue I create titled "The 30 Women Company" occurs in 1873. The setting is Cincinnati, Ohio.

2. Womxn. The term *womxn* was created to broaden the scope of the word *womanhood (women, womyn or wimmin)*. Womxn was added to Dictionary.com in 2019.

3. The refrain line of the poem, "Calling All Women" by Ruby Dee is . . . *"and bring your lunch."*

Works Cited

Dee, Ruby. "Calling All Women." *My One Good Nerve*. Wiley, 1987.
Miller Smith, Arlette. "Milk, Mothers, and Madness: Morrison's *Beloved* Women Beating Back the Past:" The 30 Women Company monologue. Unpublished.

INTRODUCTION

A number of people have asked: Why did you choose a letter-writing campaign asking women to support Senator Kamala Harris? My first reaction was to call on what I knew about the "gift" of letter writing as a power for Black women and how they wrote letters during some of the most challenging times in their lives. They wrote during their happy times and during slavery, Emancipation, and Reconstruction. And when the first Black man ran for President of the United States thereby launching a Black woman into the "first ladyship" of the country, I called for letters resulting in a book of letters for Michelle Obama. In 2012, I again called for a book of letters to support the first Black woman Superintendent of Buffalo Public Schools.

However, it came to me during the early morning hours when memories about the first letter I ever wrote as a child came flooding back. That letter was written in support of a friend. I remembered putting a stamp on the envelope and nervously dropping it in the old blue United States Postal Service mailbox on the corner of Broadway and Barnes Streets in Baltimore, Maryland. Looking back, I can describe this letter written at eleven years of age as an intervention. And that letter made its way to Harlem, New York. I was eleven or twelve when I wrote that letter, and it was on behalf of a new friend of mine who was spending the summer in Baltimore with her Aunt Mary, who lived three doors down from me. Like my family, they also lived in a rundown alley house now known as one of the famous row houses of Baltimore, still standing after the migrant Irish moved away, leaving the wreckage of the East Baltimore row house of the early 1900s, now known as the gentrified *Alley House*. But I digress!

I only remember Elaine's first name, but I remember her face and that of her mother who lost a day of work to come to Baltimore because of "my" letter. When Elaine's mother knocked on my door at 1605 Barnes Street, my mother answered. Elaine's mother thought my mother had written the letter and she asked my mother to tell her what it meant. My mother recognized my handwriting and called me inside. I saw the two of them talking about "my" letter spread out on the kitchen table. It was a long letter, but I never recalled it being so long. I was mortified. "Peggy," my mother said, "why did you write this?" I explained sheepishly. "I saw Elaine's Aunt Mary get beaten with a lead pipe and I thought Elaine wasn't safe in the house, so I wrote the letter to her mother." My mother said, "But it wasn't your business." I responded, "But I thought it was my business, and I thought Elaine's mother should know that this could also happen to Elaine." Elaine's mother asked, "Did Elaine know you had written this letter?" "Yes," I responded. "She was afraid of what I had written, but she was also afraid of Alphonso, and she went to the mailbox with me. We thought no more about it." That very night, Elaine left for Harlem with her mother and I never saw her again. Two weeks later Elaine's Aunt Mary was beaten to death with a lead pipe by Mary's husband Alphonso. That's when I started to believe in the power of letter writing. Mary was lost but Elaine was in Harlem.

Dear Kamala is one of my many forays into soliciting others to write letters. My mother inspired me to write letters, and I still remember the letters she left for her girls to read whenever she wanted to talk about a "sensitive" subject. She stuck them in the frames of the mirrors in the house. Who can pass by a mirror and not look at themselves? Always trying to guide us, she left strong messages in those brief letters like this one: "When you pass by a board with upturned nails or a broken bottle or two, do you pause for a moment to make it safe for the one who comes after you? Life could be beautiful only if we made it safe for others too, for the one you love may be the one, the one who comes after you."

Dear Kamala letter writers remind Kamala of the impressive brigade of women that she "comes after"—numerous strong, Black women community builders like Drusilla Dunjee-Houston, Mary B. Talbert, Jarena Lee, Ida B. Wells, Fannie Lou Hammer, Bernice Cannady, Elizabeth Keckley, Mary Crosby Chappell, Mollie Lee Parker Franklin—John Hope Franklin's mother, Lena Sawner, Mrs. S. Moselle, Sister Mary Carter Smith, Anna Julia Cooper, and thousands of others, and they remind her that it is her "business" to remove the "upturned nails" that disrupt this society and impede the progress of what has become a "fragile democracy."

When I first heard that Kamala Harris was going to be Joe Biden's running mate, I staggered in the knowledge that this multiethnic woman who identifies as African American would be running on the Democratic ticket and eventually emerging as Vice President of the United States, the second most powerful position on the planet! I immediately began asking women around the world to write letters to Kamala Harris sharing their thoughts, concerns, and good wishes. To my delight, they told friends and family who told other friends and their families and the letters for the book were immediate.

Ordinary women, mothers, and grandmothers and great-grandmothers responded. Young girls in a California Girl Scout troop asked to be included. Extraordinary women with a long history of supporting women in the public arena, fighting for civil rights, educating children, serving as first responders, entrepreneurs, community builders, and others. How did so many women come together for the project? This project was aided and abetted by the miracles of "social media." It must be said that the wonders of the digital world made it possible to see, talk with, and listen to women from around the world both privately and in crowded Zoom sessions attended by women representing five continents: Asia, Europe, the USA, Africa, Australia, and islands such as Madagascar, Haiti, Jamaica, and the Fiji Isles. The letters came from countries on those continents including India, Nepal, and Canada. And on the European continent, women in Sweden, England, Norway, and France responded. And women from cities in the USA from California to Virginia and Virginia to Florida and Florida to Georgia from Oklahoma to Mississippi and others also responded. Women wrote in their native tongues, for example, French and Spanish. One woman spoke Hindi but wanted help to get her letter into English. Women from the US with women friends around the world messaged their friends, coworkers, and family and informed them of the project, and they also responded.

Aside from well-wishes, these contributors were also asked to identify their chief areas of concern and how you might address them. I was particularly interested in having young people, especially young millennials to share their thoughts about you as Vice *President* of the United States. This issue brings me to another aspect of this project, which was not just an extraordinary journey but a very important one. Respondents fell into several different categories. First there are those Black women of the vast network of what are called "legacy" organizations, such as the National Negro Business Women's Clubs. This is a group of thirteen Black women's organizations with extraordinary international reach who joined me in this celebration of you, namely, the National Council of Negro Women. The NCNW is an "organization of organizations" (comprised of three hundred campus and community-based sections and thirty-two national women's organizations) that enlightens, inspires, and connects more than two million women and men.

I also noticed an absence reflected noticeably in the low number of younger Black women and women of color who responded, especially those young Black and white women whose boots are on the ground marching for George Floyd, Trayvon Martin, Freddy Grey, and Breonna Taylor. It is on this matter, Vice President Harris, that I urge you to look for those respondents who are "missing" in this dedication to you. If you look deeper, you will find that these young people signified that they were "uncomfortable" with you. That they were not satisfied with your stance on climate change and what they consider prosecutorial missteps, that they do not understand what you believe and understand about the LGBT community, that they don't accept your ideas on climate change, that they want an environment where the polar bear can have ice floes to fish from to secure food themselves and their young, that your line of prestigious memberships in Black women's organizations such as AKA impedes your understanding of the broader issues of Black women in the struggle, for example, Black Lives Matters.

I had to write these concerns in this introduction because these young women are so turned off that they did not want to write their concerns. However, despite these reservations, they thought that this election was so important that they still voted for you. I say "touché" to that.

We asked a few women and the world responded. They were from different countries with multiple backgrounds. For example, among the respondents were teachers, lawyers, historians, prosecutors, physicians, community activists, law enforcement officers, nurses, and bloggers. Many had shared similar work experiences with Kamala, like the women in the field of law from South Africa and the Ivory Coast who were Supreme Court justices in their own countries, so they understood the complexities of law enforcement and the courts. Fortunately, there were numerous independent women who were fluent in the digital world and maintained independent podcasts, blogs, and web pages. Fortunately for this project, they used their knowledge to connect with a broad audience of women who also visited #TheHarrisLettersProject and left a heavy digital footprint that benefited this effort. Such groups include BlackGirlNerds, a podcast, and WhenBlackWomenGather, a Facebook page, as well as several other individual Facebook pages.

These respondents were smitten with you, Vice President Kamala. I was struck with the casual manner in which they addressed you. They wrote as if they were speaking to you directly. Some called you Kamala, sister, and SISTAH! A number of women had met you somewhere before. And, they commended you on several fronts, for example, for having attended an historically black college, for your perseverance and your toughness and your long business, no-nonsense stride when you walk. They applauded you for your membership in various black women's organizations, especially Alpha Kappa Alpha, where many were "sorors."

The journey to put this book together brought many historical encounters to mind. For instance, my thoughts turned to Mary B. Talbert addressing the Fifth Congress of the International Council of

Women in Christiana, Norway, 1920, where she was the first African American delegate. Mary Talbert said, "The greatness of nations is shown by their strict regard for human rights, rigid enforcement of the law without bias, and just administration of the affairs of life," and this is what we are asking of you, Senator Harris: "strict regard for human rights, enforcement of the law without bias, and just administration." As one writer wrote, you can't accomplish everything but "just do no harm."

With conscious intent, Mary B. Talbert bridged the generation of nineteenth-century abolitionists and freedom seekers, racial uplift matriarchs and church builders in the Baptist church: Tubman, Douglass, Truth, and others, and the developing civil rights leadership of the twentieth century. We ask you, Vice President Kamala Harris, "to bridge with conscious intent," the generation of twenty-first-century millennials, Generation X, Y, and Z, and any of the variations thereof. Surely it's time we had "that" talk.

DEAR
KAMALA

LETTERS

Chapter 1

To Our Dear Sister Kamala,

Well, Black-woman-to-Black-woman, it's time we had "the talk." Not the talk we must have with our children about the perils of being a person of color in America, but the talk Black women must have with each other and ourselves, especially when the days get tough. It is the talk that reminds us who we are and how we are all connected as Black women. The talk to lift us up on the days when we are weary from being overlooked, underestimated, and minimized. After all, we know what you were facing as the first Black female candidate for Vice President of these United States. Regardless of political party and because we share a common belief in the goals for which you stand, as they say in the vernacular, "We Got Your Back!" We are raising our collective five million voices to uplift and encourage you. The strength and power you represent puts fear in some. When you are demeaned and disrespected, all African American women are demeaned and disrespected. We will not let this continue without a response. To the rhetoric, "angry Black woman," "monster," and other derogatory epithets hurled at you, "We Got Your Back." As any mother or sister-girlfriend would say to you and to those who would try to shut you down mentally, physically, and spiritually, ignore the chatter.

We know, and historians and archivists confirm it, the African woman is the mother of our modern civilization. For centuries, Black women have nursed and raised their babies along with the babies of others. Caring for them, encouraging them, feeding them with wonderful soulful food, using our strength to release and free others, and crying for too many lost children. It was a Black woman who was the human computer that ensured a man got to the moon. It was a Black woman, who by the strength of her will, would not be moved from her seat on a city bus and started a movement. It was a brave Black woman who took her own folding chair when she could not get a seat at any political party's table and became the first woman to run for President of these United States. And it is Black women who have raised powerful children alone and become public advocates themselves when our men of the movement are murdered. Never forget that you come from strong resilient ancestry and you will not be defeated by lies and character assassination.

We, SistersUnited4Reform, speak out to demand these attacks stop.

Sister Kamala:
Let your skills and experience be evident and never devalued as assets.
Let the power in your voice be heard and never minimized or silenced.
Let your presence be awesome but never flagrant.
Let your integrity be steadfast and never compromised.
Let your intelligence be respected and never denied.
Let your light continue to shine and never be dimmed by demagoguery, divisiveness, or delusion.
Remember . . . "We Got Your Back!"

Sisterly,
Dr. Glenda Glover, International President, Alpha Kappa Alpha Sorority, Incorporated

Beverly E. Smith, National President and CEO, Delta Sigma Theta Sorority, Incorporated

Valerie Hollingsworth Baker, International President, Zeta Phi Beta Sorority, Incorporated

Rasheeda Liberty, International President, Sigma Gamma Rho Sorority, Incorporated

Dr. Kimberly Jeffries Leonard, National President, The Links, Incorporated, and The Links Foundation, Incorporated

Dr. Johnnetta Betsch Cole, Chair and President, National Council of Negro Women

Virginia Harris, National President, National Coalition of 100 Black Women, Incorporated

Kornisha McGill Brown, National President, Jack and Jill of America, Incorporated

Margaret Gaines Clark, National President, The Girl Friends, Incorporated

Sharon J. Beard, National President, Top Ladies of Distinction, Incorporated

Melanie Campbell, President and CEO, Black Women's Roundtable

Susan Taylor, Founder and CEO, National Cares Mentoring Movement

Gwainevere Catchings Hess, President, The Black Women's Agenda, Incorporated

Chapter 2

Dear Vice President Elect Harris,

There are so many things that I want to say to you: words of encouragement, praise, advice, and warning. First, I want you to know how proud I am of you as a human being and how deserving I think you are of the honor of being nominated and elected as Vice President of the United States. Your life has been about public service, training, and preparation for this very position. You are ready for this!

Your view is global; even as a young child, you were exposed to other cultures and numerous ways of accomplishing tasks. Between two countries, you received an excellent education. You demonstrated your high capacity to learn, process, compete, and deliver. At the same time, you have seen all elements of society, from the impoverished to the very rich, from society's disenfranchised to those who are contributors, from earnest followers to motivated leaders. You have paid your dues in this arena also.

Careerwise, you worked your way up from litigator to District Attorney to Attorney General and to United States Senator. On each job, you were a change agent and a force to reckon with. When you found people who were ineffective, your goal was to improve or remove and replace. Your expectations and standards are high. You were tough on crime. Good! At the same time, you analyzed the underlying reasons for crime and sought solutions to improve the human condition. This is what we need in our country at this time.

My advice to you is to make your agenda clear. To take the phrase from the Queen of Wakanda in the movie *Black Panther*, "Show them who you are!" I understand that one has to be guarded on controversial issues. However, people want to know what your platform is so they won't be surprised later. If deep in your heart you are against capital punishment, say so. If you believe in states making case-by-case decisions, say so. No fence sitting.

You have been an advocate for women. When you cracked down on teenage prostitution in San Francisco, you made sure police treated these girls as victims and not criminals. Continue in this vein. Police reform is of paramount concern along with gun control! We don't have any more children or spouses to sacrifice. Do not be afraid to let women know that you recognize and support their right for decisions about what happens to their bodies, that you believe that they, as women, can achieve, break records and ceilings. As the child of immigrants, let your constituents know that you support the "DREAM Act," that you are against children being separated from their parents and kept in cages. This is no stretch for you—your record shows you already believe these things. On health care, let America know that you want health care for all. The greatest nation in the world needs this benefit for its citizens. You cannot go wrong by telling the truth and doing what is right for all Americans.

You will be asked tough questions but you are able to think on your feet. You are tough enough to weather the negative comments that will be thrown your way. You can articulate enough to rebuff what is being said. You have the background information to address most questions and you are a quick study. Pace yourself, take a breath, answer, doing your best with the information on hand. Walk people through your thought processes on issues that are undecided, discussing the pros and cons of an issue.

Remember, the job of a vice president in any organization is to make the President look good. You must keep him informed, give him the best advice possible, and all the while train for your next job as President. Use your influence to get Congress and the Senate to work together as Americans and for the benefit of all. They need to stop the infighting, corruption, and deal making. All of our public officials need to do the right thing because it is the right thing to keep us safe and prosperous. If they can't do that, they need to go. My prayers and thoughts are with you as you move forward in this race. I am confident you will do the best job possible.

Sincerely,
Veronica Dungee Abrams

Veronica Dungee Abrams is an AKA Soror and retired educator from the Virginia Public Schools in Fairfax County, Virginia.

Chapter 3

Dear Vice President Kamala Harris,

As I sat listening to your acceptance speech as the Democratic Party's nominee for Vice President of the United States of America in the upcoming election and then as Vice President Elect, my heart got that burst of pride that comes when one of my own children does something that makes me particularly proud to be their mother. You held your place at the podium with grace, with apparent pride in being you and with exhilaration in the anticipation of what America can be. You spoke with a voice of certainty in your belief that change must and will come in America.

America's history includes the history of the people who built this country on whose backs economic wealth was gained . . . BLACK PEOPLE! You have a fight in you that assures me that with you as vice president, we can look toward freedom and a seat at the table for our people who for so long have been overlooked, devalued, and taken for granted in this America where "white privilege" prevails. In the words of Shirley Chisholm, we can and will "bring our own folding chairs." Your attention will be on the creation of an America that adheres to the call for justice and peace for all people of this nation, so that we can truly become . . . "one nation, under GOD, indivisible, with liberty and justice for all."

Please know that this journey will not be easy . . . the opposition will try to tear you down. You will be tried as you have never been. Already people are lying about you and calling you names. Ignore them and don't buckle. Pray continuously. Speak your truth and know that we have your back. You were born for this. Carry on!

Sandra Mobley Terry Adams

Sandra Mobley Terry Adams is a retired community activist and lives in Atlanta, Georgia.

Chapter 4

Dear Vice President Harris:
Hope
Not for me
Not for you
But for us
The people
Who wish everything to just be peaceful.
Who want the good not the hate
And we are thankful for you, because you can also relate
To all the things that happened in the past that wasn't great.
To the strong African American women who look at no other
Who show respect for one another
Kamala Harris
Who fights for her rights
Each day and night
Whom I and other girls look up to
To have our country reunite
Who inspires me to try my hardest
Even when I am at my lowest
I am going to reach for my dreams because of Kamala
and not be criticized as a black girl
Cause all I want is hope.

Sincerely,
Soraya

Soraya is a ninth grader and Girl Scout from New York State. She is cocaptain of the stepping team and loves dancing and hanging out with family and friends.

Chapter 5

Dear Vice President Harris:

I call you my sister. I call you my "sistah" jubilantly. I see the shoes you are racing to fill and they are large ones. However, we are not daunted by their size or their unique style. Because we hold these truths. We held these truths. We will hold these truths.

I was born in the state of South Carolina. By the time I was five years old, we had migrated to New York State. My father was the son, grandson, and great-grandson of sharecroppers, and he needed to leave the land of red dirt and cotton fields and prejudice. For him only one of your three words mattered: community. The other two, equality and justice, must have occurred on another planet. Community for him meant family, both immediate and distant. But community was not enough to ensure his safety, so he left the South. Millions of others also left the terror of the South.

For centuries, we have counted the injustices that occurred daily in our lives and believed that perhaps the next one would be the tipping point, and that the injustices would end. We marched, we protested, we boycotted, and we gained an inch, or sometimes several inches. But inevitably we found ourselves even further behind. It is time to recover some of what we have lost. While the Presidential campaign made us hopeful, you were one among a bevy of white males (I didn't forget Booker). Then a return to two white males. Who would Biden choose? Kamala Harris. Now United States Vice President. Jubilation. Yours is the face that I see myself reflected in.

You are speaking and we are listening.

Sharon R. Amos

Sharon R. Amos, PhD, is an educator and a resident of the City of Buffalo, New York.

Chapter 6

Dear Vice President Harris:

As a Jamaican born immigrant who is also a US citizen and a person who at times stutters, I feel connected to both you (fellow Jamaican) and Joe Biden (a fellow stutterer) and was quite proud when you were named as the VP choice and then elected Vice President! I actually said it to many of my friends months ago that I think you should be the choice. Your drive, leadership, and fortitude is so needed in this country right now, and I know that you will be able to accomplish your goals despite roadblocks that will come your way. Continue to persevere. I also hope that you and Joe Biden will reestablish the President's Committee on the Arts and Humanities. As someone who works in the arts industry doing marketing for Broadway and off-Broadway productions as well as in the media and entertainment industry, it is so important to have support for these entities and we need an administration who understands its importance.

Go forth, Vice President Harris, knowing that you are supported as you lead the way and make history!

Sincerely,
Cherine E. Anderson

Cherine E. Anderson is originally from Jamaica, West Indies, and currently lives in New York City. She has worked with the television, film, theater, and entertainment industry for over twenty years and has a background in consumer and promotions marketing, partnership development, and community engagement.

Chapter 7

Dear Vice President Harris,

Congratulations on this magnificent achievement! Words cannot describe the elation of this moment in history. It shall be recognized in history forever. This is your time to shine brightly for all women all over the world. Your name will be added to the many courageous women of color who have changed the trajectory of the future for women and girls worldwide. We knew this moment would come. We stand with you in solidarity for other girls and women who are called to be of service to mankind and our country.

President Barack Obama said it best, "Change will not come if we wait for some person or some other time. We are the ones we have been waiting for. We are the change we seek."

This is your time to shine, we pray for you to have courage, wisdom, and vision for a more perfect union in these United States. Let no one diminish your light, it's your time to Shine!

With all due respect,
Dr. Gloria Anderson

Dr. Gloria Anderson currently resides in Oklahoma City, Oklahoma. She is Executive Director of a charter school and serves on several community service boards.

Chapter 8

Dear Vice President Kamala Harris,

I write this letter to you with a mixture of admiration, excitement, and great joy. You represent so much of what has been at the core of my belief system, including the values of kindness, perseverance, diligence, and generosity of spirit—and the need to believe not just in the self but also in the community. With your election, it feels that what I have worked towards in much of my life, of what I have dreamt of, and of what I want women to continue to aspire to, is about to materialize. You join the ranks of inspiring and great women, from Katherine Johnson to Barbara Jordan, to Mae Jemison and Ruth Simmons. And others.

You are no doubt aware of the auspicious burden that you now bear. For in your election rests the hopes and the dreams of so many women and girls, especially black and brown women and girls, as well as their male supporters and partners in justice and equality. In your role as Vice President, we get an inkling of what the United States *is becoming*–in the way that it was originally penned by our first African American First Lady, Michelle Obama, in her thoughtful book, *Becoming*. You have captured our country's hopes and great possibilities. Your election reminds America of what it tells itself from time to time, namely, that it is an inclusive, vibrant, beautiful, and hopeful place. You and I share a mixed racial heritage in which our blackness is at the core of our being. Like your parents, I too am an immigrant. We have also both chosen careers in the law. These remote connections with you fill me with a sense of elation and pride. I know that as Vice President you will continue to pursue the 6Rs that have been the leitmotif of your life: the respect that you give to others and that you demand from them, the resilience which has enabled you to persevere and thrive and be who you are, the rewards that you give to others and to yourself for what you deserve and what you have achieved, your fine reputation that has brought you this far, the recognition that you give *to* those who are marginalized and powerless in our society, and that you always remember where you and your people came from.

In writing this letter I yearn for the talents of a Toni Morrison or a Maya Angelou, who would wax more lyrical and provide more literary allusion. I modestly raise my glass to you, and as they say in my country of birth South Africa, Hamba Kahle; Sabia Kahle. Go well and be well.

Sincerely,
Penelope (Penny) Andrews

Penelope (Penny) Andrews lives in New York City and is Professor of Law and Co-Director, Racial Justice Project, New York Law School; Former President and Dean, Albany Law School; Former Dean, University of Cape Town, Faculty of Law.

Chapter 9

Dear Vice President Harris:

Congratulations on the achievement of a lifetime! You have the opportunity to be a light in the darkness. It is your time to shine. It is a transforming time in our nation that carries with it the weighty responsibility of healing a country suffering from a malady that is soul wrenching. America is being cleansed from the inside out. Injustice runs rampant and hatred abounds in our land. The voices of our citizens that beg solutions have been heard. You are a breath away from being the leader of the most powerful country in the world. What will you do? God knows. We don't know. I don't know.

This, I do know. The greatest power of all time is love. President Nelson Mandela discovered it. Mahatma Gandhi discovered it. Love conquers all. Look to the hills from which cometh your help. Rev. Luther Barnes' new song released in June 2020, "Look to the Hills," describes your situation perfectly. It is comforting and inspirational. Please listen to it when your needs are greatest.

As African Americans, especially women, we have a heavier load to carry, it seems. We know that we stand on the shoulders of others who endured great pain to have come this far. We must go on. I pray that you will pray for transparency as you connect the ties that bind us together in doing the hard work to help make this a more perfect union in America and, hence, advance humanity in this world. Harriet Tubman prayed. Rosa Parks prayed. Let us pray.

With all due respect,
Anita G. Arnold

Anita G. Arnold is a native Oklahoman and a veteran business owner, Real Estate Broker, Executive Director of a Black Fine Arts Institute and a retired Corporate Executive of a Fortune 500 Company and top-ranking US Postal Service Administrator. She is a community activist and served on the 1988 National Democratic Site Selection Committee, the only person from Oklahoma to have ever served on that committee.

Chapter 10

Dear Vice President Harris:

It is with pride that I am writing this letter to you.

Your becoming the Vice President of the United States of America is an outstanding achievement. It means so much in our patriarchal society. It is about time that women sit at the table. Your high achievement is a positive message for the future generations, change has come, and we, women, will make sure that nothing and nobody stops it.

Your designation is "our" designation. We are together with you. The message has traveled worldwide, we made sure of it. This election, and your new position as Vice President, for sure, will make history. We will not allow anybody to steal it from us.

The responsibility is overwhelming, but you proved to us that you can take it. We trust you on this.

Let's continue to celebrate.

Be blessed.

Dr. Nodjon Bakayoko

Dr. Nodjon Bakayoko is a dentist in the Washington, DC, metropolitan area. She has been an active activist of women's rights for many years.

Chapter 11

Très chère Kamala Harris

Vous êtes certainement surprise de recevoir une lettre en français, et du Canada. Non, je ne suis pas Américaine. Je vis au Canada et en Français. Je suis une Haïtiano-Canadienne, c'est-à-dire, une Canadienne, d'origine haïtienne. J'habite à Toronto.

Mon plaisir est tellement grand quand, à la télévision, j'ai appris que vous serez la Vice-Présidente aux côtés du M. Joe Biden aux États-Unis.

La joie de vous voir à cette position déborde les frontières américaines et voyage très loin. C'est un premier pas dans la bonne direction. C'est aussi le signal d'une inclusion qui devrait s'étendre dans tout le pays, dans toutes les directions et dans tous les champs de profession.

Toutes mes félicitations! Je vous souhaite du succès à l'élection, ce qui se matérialiserait en changement durable et continue à travers les États-Unis et au-delà.

Bonne Chance! Et Bon Succès

Jacqueline Jean-Baptiste

Dear Vice President Harris:

You may be surprised to receive a letter in French and from Canada. No, I'm not American. I have submitted my letter to you both in French and English. I am a Haitian Canadian, that is, a Canadian of Haitian descent. I live in Toronto.

My pleasure was so great when, on television, I learned that you will be the Vice President alongside Joe Biden in the United States.

The joy of seeing you at this position extends beyond the American borders and travels far away. This is a first step in the right direction. It is also a signal of inclusion that should be extended across the country, in all directions and in all fields and professions.

Congratulations! I am so thankful for your success which I hope will materialize into lasting and continuous change across the United States and beyond.

Jacqueline Jean-Baptiste

Jacqueline Jean-Baptiste was born in Haiti and currently lives in Ontario, Canada. She is an educator specializing in racism in Canada. She is also a filmmaker and was writer and director for the film *Eavesdropping on Souls: A Journey into Haitian Arts.*

Chapter 12

Vice President Kamala Harris:

It gives me great pleasure to say that! As a little girl, I remember walking to school to receive my education at a school which was in an area of the city that seemed to be reserved for people of color. Through the wind, rain, snow or sun, we walked. Until the busing started.

I remember my father coming home from the war in his uniform and the many times I ran to him when I saw him, in uniform, coming from the field where he, with other negro baseball players, had their games.

I remember standing next to my father in the surplus line, waiting to receive cheese, powdered eggs, powdered milk, and my favorite, pork 'n' beef, when an angry white man came towards me, frowned at me, and kicked the empty box that I had just rested on the floor, after having held it by my hands for hours while standing in that line. He didn't look at my father but rather kept his piercing eyes and scowling face on me. When I turned to my father to tell him that the man had kicked my box away, he simply said, "Uh-huh, uh-huh, don't say anything!" I was thirteen, tired and hungry, and could not understand why he did it and why my father allowed him to do it, without saying a word to him.

Here was a man who, I learned after he had passed, was a decorated WWII war hero, if there can be heroes in wars. The father of sixteen, twelve girls and four boys. Yet, that moment in time seemed to not matter to him, but it mattered greatly to me! It mattered because he had not, nor did he thereafter, kick anyone else's boxes which were also on the floor. And, it was that look in his eyes, that still appears in my memory today. It, to me, was the first day that I felt a feeling of disdain, of not feeling safe, of feeling I didn't belong or mattered. At the same time, I had a fierce source of strength, and remember believing that I would have to stand up for myself and what was right!

It was also that day and time that caused me to pay attention to my surroundings. I watched my mother and the other African American women of the church as the community began to stand up and organize. These strong women were working and campaigning for the Honorable Shirley Chisholm, receiving the brother of the late Medgar Evers, being sure that the children in the community got to see and hear from then Cassius Clay, who later became Muhammed Ali. They ushered us through the murder of the late Dr. Martin Luther King Jr. and the late President John F. Kennedy and so much more, while at the same time keeping their young sons and daughters right by their sides! Them teaching and us learning! I so admired my mother and her friends. They were all beautiful and the strongest African American women I knew in my young years, and so many of us wanted to be just like them!

When I look around today, many of the things in the world are the same and much is different. But one thing I know for sure is that I see the characteristics of those "Women Warriors" in you! Not afraid to ask the tough questions in order to get truthful answers, willing to serve the people and finding ways to meet their needs, answering the call to duty with a clean heart for all of God's people. Being and joining with a leader that people can follow! And, most importantly, being true to yourself and the American people, sharing a strong since of purpose, celebrating families and protecting their dreams. So, I thank you for your leadership and offer my humble encouragement for your willingness to serve in a government and as Vice President, for the people and by the people that has to come back to the people.

God's Grace and Mercy.

Always,
Crystal Barton

Crystal Barton is a high school Principal and Administrator and she lives in Niagara Falls, New York.

Chapter 13

Dear Vice President Harris:

What a joy to see you by President Joe Biden's side! I am so proud!

I canvassed in Iowa for President Obama during the second election and was happy when he won. I was living in Chicago at the time.

I voted for Mrs. Clinton and was disappointed that she did not win. Seeing a woman in your position gives me hope for all the women fighting the good fight in the world. Knowing that you could become our next President makes me optimistic. This is very promising for our future, which seems so bleak right now.

Hold on tight. The final success is near. With Joe and you in power, the Afro-American community and all the other communities will do a good job to make sure we support you in moving forward and re-becoming the United States that we've all gotten to know and cherish and help you in rebuilding a better America.

I am currently with my family in Africa (Ivory Coast), but my aunt "Khadidja Doumbia Thiam" is by your side in DC. You have all our trust.

With my best wishes, Madam Vice President,
Nina Khadidja Bassole

Nina Khadidja Bassole was born in Africa and is a Grants Management Specialist.

Chapter 14

Dear Vice President Harris,

Recently I changed what I want to be when I grow up. Just last year I decided that I wanted to do something big for the country, so I decided that I want to be a justice on the Supreme Court. Sometimes a small voice tells me that I cannot do it, that I wasn't born here in the US, and that I'm a girl. I also know there's only been two women on the Supreme Court, and I tell myself that I should forget about it and that it's not going to happen. But my feelings changed since the presidential election happened. We learned about you in school, that you are the first female Vice President and the first black Vice President too, and that inspired me and gave me courage that I can do it. It got me interested so I read more about you. I learned that you are a hard-working person, that you are determined to do your work well, commit to your assignments, and don't give up. The more I read about you my courage went up, so thank you for setting an example.

I am very happy that you and President Biden won. I believe you will be a great Vice President and I have no doubt that you will do a great job. If I could give you any advice I would say "let the haters hate" as long as you're proud of what you do and you're sure you are helping people then keep doing what you do and stride on.

I also have some questions I would love to ask you if I could. When you were little did you ever think that you would grow up to be Vice President? How do you feel about the tasks that you are going to face? And if you could change one thing about the world what would it be?

My wishes are: I hope you will stop Covid-19, I hope you will take care of our planet and stop pollution, I hope you will make sure all women have equal rights as men, I hope you can stop racism and discrimination, and I hope that you can help make a change that people that are not born in the United States can be President or have high important jobs too. And I hope to join you some day and help this country too when I grow up.

Sincerely,
Gili

Gili is a fifth grader and Girl Scout from California who loves hiking, cooking for her family, being with her friends, and playing with her dog. Gili is determined to follow her heart and be a justice in the Supreme Court, so she can help people in need.

Chapter 15

Dear Vice President Kamala,

I am writing you this letter as part of The Harris Letters Project because my mother asked me to, and she is the founder of this project. I've hesitated because I don't know what to say. I am what you might call an Afro-pessimist. I have little faith in electoral politics and view them with a high degree of skepticism. The United States is still a white settler and patriarchal colonialist project. If this weren't still the case, things would look very different than they do today. And so I regard anyone with ambitions of power within this colonialist project with a high degree of suspicion. That includes you and Joe Biden.

But my mother started this project and asked me to write a letter because she believes in something that I might not, when it comes to politics, and because she believes in the power of symbolism. In this she isn't wrong—symbols are powerful. This entire nation is built on symbols. We are fighting now over symbols—symbolic power that sometimes becomes real power. It means something that a Black woman is Vice President of this country. It means something that *any* woman could be Vice President of this country. I look around the world and see that women are in the top positions of many countries—as presidents and chancellors and prime ministers. And yet here, in seemingly the most advanced country in the world, this hasn't happened. It's simple—we are not the most advanced country in the world. We are not at the forefront. The pandemic has exposed what most of us already knew—that our symbols of freedom, equality, and achievement, are fictions. Whatever truths they might have held are steadily eroding.

And perhaps this is where you come in, to prove whether or not we can actually advance past a threshold imposed by a backward patriarchy grasping at irrelevant vestiges of power. I would not look to you or to Biden to somehow change the world merely by being in power. That's far too much and you already have so many forces arrayed against you.

What I would hope is that in the Vice Presidency you do what this current administration cannot: that you focus on doing the least amount of harm to those who are already being harmed the most, that you not only recommit to but advance the social safety nets that are crucial for this country and that have proved indispensable in other countries around the globe, and that you push for this country to rejoin the world community on crucial issues like climate change and human security. I am happy that you are now Vice President, and believe me—I hope with all my remaining hope that you know that so many are rooting for you and that it may be the most politically meaningful event to occur in their lifetimes.

In Solidarity,
Lillian-Yvonne Bertram

Lillian-Yvonne Bertram is a poet and lives in Lowell, Massachusetts. She is Associate Professor of English at University of Massachusetts. She was recently a finalist in the New York Times Book of the Year Award for her book of poems *Travesty Generator.*

Chapter 16

Dear Vice President Harris,

I see you.

I am taken back in time to the 70's, when I was just a little white girl in a predominately black east side Buffalo neighborhood. All my friends were black, but we accepted our differences, shared in our commonalities, and loved each other. I saw my friends for who they really were, bright, lively, talented, musical, energetic, loving, smart, athletic, and beautiful. We were all one group of kids loving life. As a grown, middle-class, white woman I miss that connection. I had the luxury of feeling this and knowing how wonderful life is living in harmony. Celebrating that which makes us different and embracing the love we feel when we really "see" each other is empowering. Know that we, as women of all colors, lift you, and support you in our collective journey. I hope we can see each other for who we are, strong, supportive, women.

Love,
Sarah Blawat

Sarah Blawat is a gemologist and owner of Sarah's Vintage Jewelry in Williamsville, New York.

Chapter 17

Dear Vice President Harris,

I was delighted to learn about "The Harris Letters," a project launched by a Buffalo-based scholar and educator named Dr. Peggy Brooks-Bertram, because your service *"for the people"* has put so much "wind beneath the wings" of so many folks, including myself!

Though I am a white woman, I am a staunch Democrat who knows and understands that Black women are our most educated, pragmatic, and dedicated voters. I cheered your Presidential campaign because your presence on the trail forced our still very white and very male mainstream media to *finally* focus on the needs and concerns of Black women. I loved when you spoke about being able to imagine what could be without being encumbered by what has always been. I cried when you ended your campaign, because I worried after the historic, barrier-breaking Presidency of Barack Obama and the popular vote win of Secretary Hillary Clinton and wondering whether America would never be ready again for another President who *wasn't* cis, hetero, white, and male.

I never gave up on the notion that you would still be in the mix, though! In fact, I left my "Kamala Harris For the People" lawn sign up all winter and added a "Biden for President" next to it, in hopes Vice President Joe Biden would choose *you* as his running mate. I am happy to report that I cried *joyful* tears when Vice President Biden announced that you *would* be joining his ticket as *his* Vice President and even more tears when you became Vice President Elect!!

Your story—your family's story—*is* the American dream. It means the world to BIPOC and to every other "marginalized" group you have ever championed to know they will have an ally and an advocate in the White House. I think especially of all of the young Black women, the young South Asian women, the young immigrants, watching you on TV, seeing "She the Vice President" in action, knowing they too, can ascend to such heights someday.

Finally, I want to let you know how many folks you have cheering for you online. I know you know the #KHive (and #DougHive!) are in your corner and we are *ride-or-die*! Spending my time parsing the ups and downs of the cruel, inhumane Trump Presidency, and the joyful happenings of your campaign with these folks has been one of the brightest spots in the past four years and I thank you for inspiring us to coalesce around you every day.

In Buffalo, the "underdog" city where I lived for 15+ years, we boost our city and our brethren and sistren by talking about "Buffalove." When I think and talk about what *your* service has meant to me and to my friends in #KHive, I use the word "Kamalove."

Thank you so much, Vice President Harris. You and Joe Biden defeated Donald Trump and the GOP—and white supremacy!—in November 2020. Stay healthy and safe!

Best,
Stacey Bowers

Stacey Bowers lives in Sanborn, New York, with her husband and numerous pets. She has a Master of Information and Library Science from Pratt Institute in Brooklyn, New York. She works for a small Irish company, where she manages a team of eight subject-matter experts researching, identifying, and reporting on product compliance obligations for retailers and manufacturers globally.

Chapter 18

Dear Vice President Harris:

Congratulations on your election as Vice President of the United States. I am especially impressed with your involvement with and support of women's organizations across the country. As you know, the record of African American women and their contributions to the building of this country plays a critical role in the education of the entire country. This is especially true of those "early" African American women pioneers who escaped slavery and survived Emancipation, Reconstruction, and the civil rights struggles in this country.

I am writing this letter to you as President of the Uncrowned Queens Institute for Research & Education on Women Inc. Since 2001, this institute has been the premier online organization researching, documenting, and preserving the regional histories of African American women and men in Western New York and across this nation. Still dedicated to its original mission, and still growing, the Institute entered its second decade in 2019 and is still dedicated to this important mission.

The Institute was initially established as a project of the City of Buffalo's Women's Pavilion, Pan Am 2001 Celebration. Originally, the goals of the Institute were to commemorate the history of African and African American women and their involvement in the Pan American Exposition of 1901. It grew from this initial focus to recognize, celebrate, and document the accomplishments and contributions of African American women during that period and in the one hundred years after the Pan American Exposition. It quickly became clear that the efforts to collect, disseminate, and archive the histories of African American women for the Buffalo Women's Pavilion very quickly morphed into a "regional" undertaking and that it told a regional history that would also encompass the histories of African American men and numerous community organizations. It became not only a regional history project requiring a sustainable organization but also rapidly required an online presence at uncrownedqueens.com and uncrownedcommunitybuilders.com to respond to worldwide requests for information.

The Institute's name, Uncrowned Queens, was derived from the 1917 poem, "America's Uncrowned Queens," by Oklahoma pioneer and poet, Drusilla Dunjee Houston. The poem celebrates "a group of tireless, self-sacrificing black women who worked for the betterment of family and community." In 2003, the Institute was formally recognized as a 501 c (3) organization by the Internal Revenue Service.

It is my hope that in your new post as Vice President, you will quickly establish a task force to identify, listen to, and formulate policies to assist community-based organizations that need ongoing support to continue their work in documenting the history of African American women in this country. I am very enthusiastic about your success and your new position as Vice President of the United States of America.

Peggy Brooks-Bertram

Peggy Brooks-Bertram, DrPH, PhD, lives in Buffalo, New York, and is a historian, President of the Uncrowned Queens Institute for Research and Education on Women Inc., and CEO of Jehudi Educational Services.

Chapter 19

Dear Vice President Kamala Harris:

I would like to offer and extend to you my warmest and most sincere congratulations as the first woman of color as the Vice President. As you begin your journey and take on these next steps in your career, just know that the leadership process will not be easy but through faith, hope, and effective prayer, all things are possible to them that believe (Mark 9:23, King James version). Faith is the substance of things hoped for and the evidence of things not seen (Hebrews 11:1, King James version).

Your leadership attributes and inspiration are something that we look forward to you sharing. Your smile says it all without saying one word. Be strong and of a good courage . . .

(Deuteronomy 31:6, King James version). Keep that beautiful smile glowing for all the world to see.

Sincerely,
Dr. Zeldra M. Bryant, EdD, MBA, BS/BA

Dr. Zeldra M. Bryant is the Deputy Director of Black Liberated Arts Center Inc. in Oklahoma City, Oklahoma.

Chapter 20

Dear Vice President Harris:

I recall preparing for my move to California late May of 2014. My grandmother says to me, "Get to know who's in charge (politicians) and their views. You need to know right away who is doing what for 'our' people and the community you live in." In all honesty, I had no idea who Kamala Harris was. She was at that time the District Attorney of San Francisco. I was moving to Sacramento. Well it wasn't very long before I got to know this representation of me. I saw and heard in you, Kamala Harris, the precision in your speech, the steadfastness in your decisions; and you just exuded confidence when you talked. I was impressed, to say the least.

When the 2017 elections came around and I had become very familiar with the views of those seeking office, I already knew that you were my choice for California State Senate. Now, oh wow, how much more overjoyed am I that you have been elected Vice President. I had tears streaming down my face and I said "For such a time as this! Yessssss!" Thank you for accepting the nomination and being ready for such a time as this! Thank you for steadying the mirror for Black Women as myself.

Sincerely,
Joylette Bullock

Joylette Bullock lives in Baltimore, Maryland, and is an Administrator at the Department of Justice in Maryland.

Chapter 21

Dear Vice President Harris,

"For everything there is a season . . ."

Congratulations on your historic nomination for Vice President of the United States of America and finally being elected as Vice President. The weight of your nomination hit me as you gave your acceptance speech during the Democratic National Convention. Thank you for calling out the names of a few of the strong, determined women who made a difference in shaping American history and recognizing that each paved a way for you in this season.

How appropriate that your nomination and your election as Vice President came during the 100th anniversary of the 19th Amendment which granted women the right to vote. In addition to Mary Church Terrell, whose name you called—I also call upon the other African American suffragists of the time—Frances Ellen Watkins Harper, Mary Ann Shadd Cary, Nannie Helen Burroughs, and Ida B. Wells. May they further inspire and guide you through your journey. Thank you for our introduction to Kamala Harris, controlling your narrative in your voice. Embracing your heritage and your life experiences, you dashed the rumors of the naysayers who obviously didn't know. They didn't know your character. They didn't know your strength. They didn't know your tenacity.

We learned of your love of family in all the forms that have shaped your journey. May they all continue to surround you with love and support. I, along with many other women, stand to be part of your new family. We, too, support and defend you. In this chaotic time, I look forward to you standing with Joe Biden to heal the divisiveness and hurt the country is currently experiencing. Not only do I look forward to saying Vice President Kamala Harris, it pleases me that generations will learn of your accomplishments.

One Love,
Sandra Williams Bush

Sandra Williams Bush lives in Buffalo, New York, and is a retired Librarian.

Chapter 22

Dear Vice President, Kamala:

I am one more woman among the millions who was enthusiastic about your candidacy for Vice President and then your selection by the American people to serve as Vice President. You brought added intelligence, knowledge, and energy to the Democratic ticket, a ticket that had to win. Nothing less than the welfare of the planet was at stake.

Trump focused his assaults on the Democratic ticket on you. You easily outshone Trump and Pence, both in your knowledge of the issues as well as in providing reasonable explanations to support the priorities of the Democratic ticket.

Considering what was at stake in the election, you were and are under considerable pressure. You will make some mistakes. Do not think about them. Just continue to move forward. Do not let accusations connected with being a prosecutor affect you. You were doing a necessary and important job. You were not responsible for the laws. As Vice President, your job is concerned with the broader needs of our society.

You have done well. I feel very hopeful that you will be a very successful Vice President, of whom Americans will be proud.

Very truly yours,
Louise E. Carey, JD

Louise E. Carey, JD, is a semiretired practicing attorney and she lives in Buffalo, New York.

Chapter 23

Chère Madame Vice-présidente élue,

C'était tellement réconfortant de vous voir, vous et votre mari, lors de votre discours d'acceptation. La vision de la solidité que vous représentez vous-même et votre couple me semble être le symbole d'une nouvelle ère pour l'Amérique. Comme l'a dit la mairesse de Paris «Bienvenue de retour l'Amérique».

Je suis tellement touchée que nous ayons tant de choses en commun. N'est-ce pas ce que la plupart des gens essaient de faire avec les autres? Voir ce qui les unit ou les divise? Je vois que vous et votre gouvernement recherchez l'unité plutôt que la division et cela me plaît. Je suis née à Poughkeepsie New York et mes parents m'ont toujours dit à quel point ils aimaient l'expérience qu'ils avaient vécue avec des Américains de toutes cultures dans les nombreuses villes où ils vivaient, alors que mon père y était psychiatre, avant de retourner au Québec où mes frères et moi avons grandi. J'ai appris que vous aviez grandi/ fréquenté l'école à Montréal avant de déménager aux États-Unis.

De plus, nos maris sont tous deux ouverts et soutiennent notre carrière, tout en maintenant une carrière très réussie de leur côté. Cela crée par l'exemple de bons changements dans nos communautés et dans le monde. J'ai des frissons en vous écrivant cette note, Kamala et au premier « second gentlemen » des États-Unis.

Ensemble, vous allez changer la façon dont les Américains et les entreprises américaines voient les femmes et les minorités en position de leadership. Le monde entier aura les yeux tournés sur M Emhoff et ses qualités de leadership. Ce sera une ère passionnante pour l'Amérique du Nord et les relations entre le Canada et les États-Unis.

Encore une fois mes félicitations les plus cordiales et au plaisir de vous voir œuvrer au sein de la communauté mondiale,

Geneviève Carle, MBA, PMP

Chère Madame Vice President,

It was so heart-warming to see you and your husband at your acceptance speech. The vision of solidity you yourself and your couple represent seems to me to be the symbol of a new era for America. As the mayoress of Paris said "Welcome back, America."

I am so touched that we have some things in common. Isn't that what most people try to do with others? See what unites or divides them? I see you and your government looking for unity vs. division and that pleases me. I was born in Poughkeepsie, New York, and my parents always talked to me about how they loved the experience they had with Americans from all cultures in the many towns they lived in while my father was a psychiatrist there, before they moved back to Québec where my brothers and I grew up. I learned that you grew up/ went to school in Montreal before moving to the states.

Both of our husbands are very open and supporting of our careers, even while having a successful career of their own. This is creating good changes in our communities and in the world, leading by example.

I have chills as I am writing this note to you, Kamala, and to the first second gentleman of the United States. Together, you are going to change how Americans and corporate America see women leaders and minorities and everyone will have eyes on Mr. Emhoff and his leadership qualities. This is going to be an exciting era for North America and the Canada–USA relationship.

Warm regards and again congratulations,
Geneviève Carle

Geneviève Carle, MBA, PMP, has more than 25 years of experience in strategic, organizational, and operational consulting with top multisites and multidisciplinary teams and leaders across the country. She lives in Sainte-Julie, Québec, Canada.

Chapter 24

Dear Vice President Harris,

Congratulations on becoming the first female Vice President! This shows that women can do anything and maybe one day I will be Vice President, too. And it is about time that a person of color was elected Vice President. It makes me sad that people would treat someone differently just because of a color.

As a kid, did you ever dream about being the Vice President of the United States? Were you ever a Girl Scout? My Girl Scout leader is teaching us a lot about endangered animals critical to our ecosystem, and that is one of my concerns for the future. Our Girl Scout troop is selling chocolates and nuts to help save the pygmy sloths. The money we raise will help plant trees for the sloths to live in.

If you could change one thing in our country, I would want it to be helping the homeless. I see a few homeless people in my community, and they look sad and hungry and I wish we could help them. For example, I think you could make more buildings (like a free hotel) for them to live in.

One piece of advice I would give you is do not listen to people who say you can't do it. If you just believe in yourself, you can make it happen. Thank you for opening lots of doors for girls like me.

Sincerely and from my heart,
Irelyn

Irelyn is a fifth grader and Girl Scout from California, and likes gymnastics, baking, and reading.

Chapter 25

Dear Vice President Harris,

That Little Girl Was [ALSO] Me.

All of us little girls and boys felt your words deeply that night during the debate when you addressed the issue of bussing. The memories came pouring back for us. Whether we were bussed to "nicer" schools in "better" neighborhoods with newer books, or, as in my case, sent to a less affluent part of town. In 1967 my classmates and I left an extremely high-achieving school with record attendance levels and we were sent to a run-down, low-achieving school. This school was selected purely based on skin color. It was predominantly white, therefore, it had to be better . . . right?

Color, as we have observed over the years can camouflage truth. It can hide ignorance yet expose hypocrisy. Your challenges are great. But just as you survived the challenges of bussing, you are up for the challenges that lie ahead. You have gained respect from many factions of this democracy, the democracy that is crumbling, the democracy that we are valiantly trying to save. But more importantly, more significantly, more urgently, you have displayed a strong sense of pride, self-assurance, and self-confidence, which prepares you for the road ahead. The words that will be used to dishonor you, to discredit you will not negatively affect your determination. Words cannot harm those who have the courage to fight for what is right, for what is decent.

My father was a college graduate (HBCU) as were his parents, my mother and her parents. My father used to say, "Just do the right thing, just do what's right." When you do what is right, cowards will melt before you. Naysayers will hide in shame and racists will creep back into the basements and backyards from whence they came because doing what's right gives you the strength to stand tall in your determination, fortitude, and brilliance. And all of us, sisters, brothers, and admirers, will stand and guard beside, ahead of, and behind you. Your role is vital to our survival, and no one is better equipped to lead us. Thank you for your sacrifice.

Blessings, Love and Support,
Soror Patrice Cathey

Soror Patrice Cathey lives in Buffalo, New York, and is part of the AKA Legacy.

Chapter 26

Dear Kamala,

It is an honor to have this opportunity to write you this personal letter from Pittsburgh, Pennsylvania. Your election as Vice President brings great hope to our nation. You, as an African American and South Asian American woman, and as a former district attorney, Attorney General, Senator, and now as Vice President, have opened doors to shine a bright light for all women and little-girl dreamers around the world. You have shown women and girls that their dreams can become a reality.

I, too, am an African-American woman, and I can certainly identify with the challenges and struggles that you have faced in your professional career. In the early 1970's I worked with community-based organizations to advance housing and community development in struggling urban neighborhoods. In the early 1980s I developed a non-profit advocacy organization to combat housing discrimination and advance fair housing in Western Pennsylvania. That advocacy organization still exists today. In the late 1990s and until my retirement, I worked in housing and civil rights for the US Department of HUD. I know the trials and tribulations of a woman's journey, particularly for women of color who fight for social justice, equality, and advancements for all.

We are living in difficult times, but your election as Vice President gives me hope for change. We need your help more than ever. We need your strength, your perseverance, and your integrity to help solve our nation's complex social issues. We know that you will fight "the good fight" for justice and equality. We know that you will stand and speak out for women's rights. We know you will work hard to tear down barriers to opportunities that exist for so many American and immigrant families.

In 1963, James Baldwin thought that Martin Luther King's dream could be fulfilled if we all worked together. Baldwin said, "The country will now go to work, and very hard work, very dangerous work, to change itself." In 2020 many of us are ready for this job, and I want you to know that we are with you. During your toughest moments, I hope that these personal letters will inspire you and give you joy on our journey to many victories. With love and hope, I leave you with warmest regards.

Donna C. Chernoff

Donna C. Chernoff lives in Pittsburgh, Pennsylvania.

Chapter 27

Dear Vice President Harris,

I am so honored to have the opportunity to write to you! It is extraordinary because you are on the executive branch, and you are the first female vice president! I am personally a little surprised that a woman would be Vice President, since men have continuously been President and Vice President. I really wish that girls had been accepted and taken equally earlier. All the books that I read normally have the women or girls folding laundry, or cooking, but never hunting or fishing or running. And even now, there is still some sexism. I hope that since you are Vice President, you will be able to change that. I also hope that I get to meet you one day!

I wonder, how do you feel about how the country is run right now? What do you do as Vice President? If you could change one thing for our country, please make sure that everyone gets an education, whether they are a girl, a boy, American, Japanese, Mexican, or Indian. I think that everyone has a right to be taught by teachers and learn.

I also think that America needs to work on driving less and stopping the spread of pollution. Maybe we could have a holiday where people try to stop using gasoline? Global warming is getting very dangerous for polar bears and arctic animals because the glaciers are melting. If global warming keeps up, Polar bears will be extinct. Also because of all the trash we throw in the ocean, sea creatures' homes are being destroyed and turtles are being killed because they think that plastic bags are jellyfish.

I am an animal lover and I think that people should try to save all animals. We should take helpless animals from kill shelters and bring them to safe shelters. We should make sure that animals are safe, healthy, and in their right habitat.

Sincerely,
Eleanor

Eleanor is a fifth grader and Girl Scout from California. She loves soccer, fashion designing, and writing.

Chapter 28

Dear Vice President Harris,

I am very honored to have this opportunity to write to you! It is outstanding that you are the first female Vice President of color. I wonder what would you do if you could change one thing about this world? I also wonder how it feels being the Vice President. If I were the Vice President, I would prioritize pollution and equality as my main priorities.

I think you should try and stop pollution because trash is clogging up the oceans and is destroying the homes of many sea creatures. Also, pollution is contaminating the skies, more and more glaciers are melting, and arctic animals are in danger. Some ideas are to try to get people to stop using gasoline, use less trash, and make more reusable necessities for people, because then they won't waste so much plastic.

Girls and women are still being treated unfairly. Many men expect women to clean the dishes, cook dinner, and take care of children. I think women and men should be treated equally. I think women and girls should be able to think for themselves and make their own decisions.

Sincerely,
Mikaela

Mikaela is a fifth grader and Girl Scout from California. She loves art, animals, and playing with her pet dog Hugo.

Chapter 29

Hello Vice President Harris:

Just wanted to drop a quick line in support of your historic run as our first woman and woman of color to be nominated as the Vice President of the United States (VPOUS) and you won! Congratulations! As a sixth-generation African American woman, an HBCU graduate, and an aspiring grass roots politician, I am excited and elated to witness and support such an awesome achievement.

I wish you all the best and am rooting for your success. Keep your head up and in the game to WIN. God Bless!

Sincerely,
Tischa Cockrell

Tischa Cockrell is a Dayton, Ohio, native and currently resides in Washington, DC, where she serves as an Advisory Neighborhood Commissioner (ANC). She is a graduate of the Catholic University of America and Central State University in Wilberforce, Ohio.

Chapter 30

Dear Vice President Harris:

As a politician myself, it is with a sincere satisfaction that I have accepted to write you a letter of support. Our world needs women in power to make sure that a decent order in the social and political environments can be established.

It is not an easy task to be in the political arena as a woman, and I know that you will need strength and patience to prevail and you will. I have been following your activities with attention since you were nominated as a Vice Presidential candidate. I am delighted that the Biden-Harris team won this election, for the good of the United States and, also, for the rest of the world. Stay strong because you are a winner and, women around the world are ecstatic about the good results of this election and that we can celebrate it with you.

God bless you!
Mrs. Boundou Coulibaly

Mrs. Boundou Coulibaly is a politician and a member of the "Bureau Politique," the highest level of the PDCI-RDA, the oldest party in the Ivory Coast. Mrs. Coulibaly is a businesswoman and worked as a Deputy Mayor until 2018 when she resigned.

Chapter 31

Well, greetings to the new Vice President:

I am so excited to let you know I sing your praises and am grateful for the God-given privilege to see the first female of color as the new Vice President of the United States. Your beautiful smile is reflected in the television cameras, and your eloquent speeches make any girl or woman of color so proud to be brown.

I know you are going to light up the White House with your grace, smiles, and presence. I shed tears of joy, emotions of hopefulness, heart of love, and prayers of thankfulness and peace for the world. My entire being believes wholeheartedly that your candor, professionalism, and calmness is what our world yearns for in this unsettled environment in which we live. You will help bring peace and love and restore some balance in these most difficult times. Our history will have a story to tell and you will be in the highlights.

My prayer is that you stay safe, well, and as you always are, graceful, calm, and professional. I look forward to seeing you in the White House. You have cheerleaders and I'm amongst the biggest. My prayers are with you, your family, and the world.

Sisterly,
Gladys Jean Diji

Gladys Jean Diji, MSN, RN FCN, is an Adjunct Clinical Professor, School of Nursing at D'Youville College, Buffalo, New York.

Chapter 32

Dear Vice President Harris,

I have American and Indian roots and live in California. I enjoy politics and love playing "270 to Win," which is a website that lets you play with the electoral map. I was ecstatic when you won and could not stop screaming. I hope this makes you smile.

I think it is so cool that a woman has finally become the Vice President. I think that it means that the country is one step closer to gender equality. You have also set an example for me and the rest of the girls in America. I hope when we grow up that people like you are everywhere. You have inspired me and the girls in my troop.

I admire how you stick it out even when things get tough, and I wanted to ask you how you managed it. What do you do when things get tough?

What is one message you could give to a girl like me? I am sure whatever the message, many, many girls around the country would treasure it. I know I will.

Sincerely,
Kiana

Kiana is a member of a Girl Scout troop and lives in California. She plays soccer, loves traveling to different places, and loves to experiment with anything (even food!!).

Chapter 33

Dear Vice President Harris:
In January 2017 women had one dream,
A dream to get their comrades elected.
A dream where women will take power,
It felt like a dream.
October 2017, the Democratic party won back Virginia.
It was the beginning of the triumph.
Women working on the ground made it happen.
When women vote we win.
August 2020, a woman is a vice presidential candidate.
The Democratic party did it again.
She is bright, educated, powerful, dedicated,
A woman of the 21st century
Above all SHE IS A WOMAN
And she is a "colored" woman
Of all colors.
She is telling all women that
We all have a seat at the table.
What a heavy responsibility!
Too many expectations.
But at the end we all win
Our dream came *through*.
Let's support the woman
Let's not ask for too many things
She knows what we need.
She won't be able to do it all.
But she will try her best.
Let's not support her for a specific purpose
Let's support KAMALA HARRIS
A WOMAN

The woman who is making history.
We are making history.
Joe Biden,
You are a wise man,
You understand what the time is.
This is what a politician, a diplomat, a smart individual does.
Let's keep on dreaming
A woman at the White House, one day,
We had a dream,
We, women, will not be stopped from now.

Kadidia Doumbia

Kadidia Doumbia was born in France. She is a Specialist in Gender and Education and an International Baccalaureate Examiner and is the District of Columbia Human Rights Liaison.

Chapter 34

Dear Vice President Harris:

During the past 11 years I have presented roses to notable women in our community here in Western New York. The Awards program is called "Roses for Outstanding Women." I have included the following statement on the front of the program booklet: "Roses are known for their great beauty and they have a special place in our lives. Like a rose, a woman is special at any age. Roses come in many colors, but the red rose stands out from all the rest. All of the women honored are like these special flowers. They stand out in our community and touch so many lives in so many ways." Although I can't see you in person, I wish to present you with the Roses for Outstanding Women Award in recognition of your contributions, talent, knowledge, and tremendous leadership. You are an inspiration to women everywhere and to our young girls who need to see the images of powerful black women who stand out and who make a difference for us all. Women like you encourage us all to be our very best and to reach for the stars.

When I see you and hear you speak, I am reminded of so many Black women from the past and present who stand out among us. I once wrote an article entitled "A Tribute to Women of Greatness." The goal of this article was to lift up our women and to give them the appreciation for their contributions to our community and to the nation. It was a celebration of women. This letter is a tribute to you, Vice President Harris, as a woman of strength and greatness. We need your leadership and your guidance in this time of uncertainty in our nation.

You have joined the list of Black women who gave us their wisdom, creative energy, leadership, talent, and great power. And like Shirley Chisholm, who cracked that glass ceiling so many years ago, you are just as "Unbought and Unbossed." We love you for it. We honor you for it.

In tribute to you the words of the poet Maya Angelou come to mind when she wrote Phenomenal Woman. My sister Vice President Kamala Harris—that's You.

Sincerely,
Dr. Eva M. Doyle

Dr. Eva M. Doyle is a long-time community journalist and a community historian in Buffalo, New York.

Chapter 35

Dear Vice President Harris:

In this difficult Covid 19 pandemic era, the announcement of your nomination as the Vice Presidential Democratic candidate was refreshing and exalting. And, now to know that you and Joe Biden have won the White House, I am ecstatic. Since January 2017, women in this country have strived to have their acquired rights maintained and respected. The actual administration is threatening us, every day, to take them from us.

Black women in this country have shown that they can make a difference and they do make a difference in all elections, nowadays. We made a difference for you. Women went out to vote to make sure that you would be whom you are supposed to be: the most powerful woman on earth. We, women, especially black women, did not fail you.

I am keeping you in my prayers. You need to be strong.

We have your back. I have your back.

Sincerely,
Micheline Ewang

Micheline Ewang lives in Silver Spring, Maryland. She is a singer and political activist.

Chapter 36

Dear Madam Vice President,

Congratulations! With your election as Vice President of the United States of America, we are entering another historic moment in our Nation. It has been a pleasure to witness your journey on your way to this new position and to witness the faith that the American people have placed in you. Your vast political experience has already taught you that you must remain vigilant to meet the new challenges that you will face every day. You are truly an inspiration and a role model for countless young women and men around the world.

As you join the President in governing our Nation, please be aware that most Americans will realize that you will continue to work to keep America strong for all of us, and they will stand beside you. Having lived and traveled up and down the West Coast, the East Coast—including the District of Columbia—and the heartland, I have observed that most people need and want the same basic things above all else. They need employment to be able to feed, clothe, house, and educate their families and to keep them safe and healthy. They want a democratic government. They also want an American identity and a relationship with the rest of the world of which they can remain proud. All of the many issues that we face in our Nation today arise from these basic needs and wants. I look forward to your governance for years to come.

Sincerely,
Betty K. Falato

Betty K. Falato retired from Federal Aviation Administration Headquarters in Washington, DC, as a senior system engineer for the National Airspace System. She lives in Norman, Oklahoma.

Chapter 37

Dear Vice President Harris:

I am very happy and proud of you. You are a role model for all women in a society where the position of women is not appreciated at its true value. Women have fought and are still fighting for their rights and respect, but there is still work to be done. We are in a new era of our civilization, and with the pandemic the challenge is even greater than ever.

To have you, a woman, at this level in the political arena is such a huge symbol for me.

Hard work always gives the right result. We are counting on you to carry the torch even higher.

Be assured that you can count on me and on millions of women to support you.

Congratulations!

Ariane Foadé

Ariane Foadé is a painter from Canada with roots in the Ivory Coast in West Africa. She lives in Montréal, Quebec.

Chapter 38

Dear Kamala:

I am calling you by your first name because I feel that I know you. In our cultures, children and strangers never address adults in the familiar without permission. How many times have I had to gently remind some white person of that fact when they dared to call me by my first name? So-o-o, that only leaves a second and different fact. You are family. Simple. It's a cultural thing. As such we owe you loyalty. You already have our deepest respect. You are not alone. We love you and worked hard to get you and Joe through the White House door. We made it! Thank you for being our inspiration and a model of great integrity.

Aisha-Sky Gates

Aisha-Sky Gates is a relationship coach and writer. She lives in a small town in Massachusetts and enjoys rural life.

Chapter 39

Dear Vice President Harris:

It was late in the evening when the Swedish news broadcast announced that Joe Biden selected Sen Kamala Harris to be his running mate in the upcoming Presidential elections. I woke up the next morning and asked my Swede if I had been dreaming. He confirmed that it did indeed happen and I broke into a happy dance! My HU (Howard University) Bison alumnae and sister in the "Divine 9" was making history by becoming the first Black/Indian woman Vice-Presidential candidate on a major political party ticket. While I had already been working on Get Out The Vote efforts with Democrats Abroad/Global Black Caucus, this announcement gave me new impetus to reach as many overseas Americans as possible. Our votes mattered. Our votes were the margin of victory in key states. Members of the Divine 9 around the world were excited. I've talked to some of them. They all wanted to see Senator Harris take her rightful place. Black Women Vote and made sure we did in this historic election. When you called out Howard University and the Divine 9 in your acceptance speech, my heart burst with pride. Go Kamala! Go Bison! HU, you know!

Adrianne George

Adrianne George is a Washington, DC, native who splits her time between western Sweden and Washington, DC. She is a member of the Democratic National Committee representing Democrats Abroad, serving a term from 2016 to 2024.

Chapter 40

Dear Vice President Harris,

I am so proud of you! You gave this Louisiana girl a chance to see a woman of color become Vice President of the United States and, maybe, the future POTUS!

Oh, how I wish my mom was here so I could share the good news with her. You see, my mom was a great role model for my sisters and me. She always sang the praises of strong Black women, as I perceive you to be. Another strong Black woman I perceived as a role model, when I was young, was the political giant from Texas, Ms. Barbara Jordan.

Ms. Jordan was very smart and wise. I was captivated with the presentation of her arguments and the efficient organization of her thoughts. It was fascinating to listen to her speak during the Congressional Hearings of Watergate. Her voice alone demanded attention. Like you, she was a lawyer, an educator, and a civil rights activist. Like you, she wore many other hats as well. In one interview, Ms. Jordan was asked if she felt her work was just for Black folks—she said no. She believed that wherever she was present, Black folks were present. They were "there." The need for us to be present, to be "there" is the key!

So, in this historical moment, I am glad you are there. Your accomplishments are celebrated by my four sisters and at least three of my four brothers. And for all I know, my two brothers and one sister, who have passed on, are also celebrating. Your nomination would definitely be celebrated by Lillie Mae and Lawrence Gordon Sr., our parents, who grew up through the depression and wartime. My parents raised twelve children in the deep South through the Jim Crow years, the Civil Rights movement, desegregation, and into an era where they believed things were going to be much better for Black folks. They felt their children and grandchildren would have opportunities in education, housing, careers, sports, etc. to achieve their dreams. An exciting first was watching my parents participate in government with the passing of the Voting Rights Act in the late '60s. These basic freedoms/rights were finally being realized. But here we are today, living through the powerful movement of Black Lives Matter. We have got to keep this moving forward. We must solidify equal rights for people of color, poor people, LGBTQ, etc. who continue the struggle against the current administration that is working to erase gains made during the Civil Rights movement.

My family and I celebrate your nomination and your ascension to the Vice Presidency. We believe you will represent all people well. You are smart and you have gained valuable experience through years in government. You are wise from your experiences and you know what you are about to face. I hope this letter is one of many that will lift you as you soar on your journey and that it will buffer your wings as you deal with the turbulence you expect as you fight for our democracy. Stay strong! Stay safe! It is so very important that you are there! Congratulations!!

Sincerely,
Theresa Gibbs

Theresa Gibbs is a retired teacher and lives in Central New Jersey in Holmdel.

Chapter 41

Queen, and Vice President Harris:

Do not worry
about anyone
taking your
CROWN.
Crowns are a Gift
from God, they are
custom made.
Your Crown will
NEVER FIT
ANYONE ELSE
Queen Harris
I was born black
and I will die black
I just don't want to
die because I am black.

Linda Gillespie

Linda Gillespie makes her home in Fresno, Texas.

Chapter 42

Dear Vice President Harris:

My heart is overjoyed and I am beyond proud of what all of your #BlackGirlMagic has achieved!! Achieving the status of Democratic nominee for Vice President and then becoming Vice President of the United States was not easy. Please take time for self-care and pat yourself on the back for a job well done. Although the job has hardly just begun! There will be opposition along the way and people may not always agree but keep pressing. I listened to you on National Public Radio when you were running for President and I was very impressed by how strong you stood by policy recommendations even though they may not have been popular nor pleasing to every demographic.

Last year I too ran for political office. I ran for Councilmember of the Masten District in Buffalo, NY. There were none and still are no women in any of the nine Councilmember districts here. I have served the community for many years and I felt my education, volunteer activities, and work experience qualified me to move forward in government but it did not happen. Even though I didn't win I know I was brave and was told by many that I was an inspiration. I feel the same way about you. I am sure you are well aware of the opposition that is to come during the campaign season and while in office and yet like Shirley Chisolm you are still demanding your seat at the table. Salute!

As a professional Black Woman with my Master's degree in Social Work I fully grasp a holistic approach to many of the inequities in our society and I hope that you appoint someone along the way who also has a degree in Social Work. My greatest drive is to not become a statistic and I know that success is a possibility with the right support and resources along the way. I know that you also understand the role politics play in providing and allocating resources.

No matter the opposition, you are a winner because of the hard work and perseverance that has propelled you to be a success despite personal and societal obstacles thus far. May the wonderful opportunity you have to build relationships and educate people on diversity be a part of your legacy. I join you in full support. You are the best choice for Vice President. I will be praying for you and sending you love from afar. Thank you so much for breaking barriers and fiercely going after your goals so that the world may benefit!

With Love,
Veronica Golden

Veronica Golden is a resident of Buffalo, New York. She is a member of the Buffalo Association of Black Social Workers and a graduate of the Women Elect program, which educates and empowers women to run for political office. She has been elected to the Erie County Democratic Committeeman seat and in 2019 was a candidate for the Buffalo City Council.

Chapter 43

Dear Vice President Harris:

Sending warm greetings from Hollywood, FL. Like you, I'm a woman who has crossed cultures, marrying a man of a different race and ethnic background. This was something my parents, civil rights and peace activists, like your own, taught me to be open to as well

We are counting on you to represent the underrepresented, the quiet voices of tolerance, and to reaffirm the strength in all forms of diversity in our country. We want you to know that we appreciated your courage and conviction to run in what was a truly challenging race.

We admire your intellect and debating prowess and count on you to defeat the forces of ignorance, intolerance, bigotry, and racism and to make the climate and our planet a priority.

We're so proud of you and look forward to calling you OUR Madame Vice President!

Namaste and many blessings,
Dr. Donna Goldstein

Dr. Donna Goldstein is a resident of Hollywood, Florida. "Dr. Donna" is a 30-year veteran psychologist, former Corporate Wellness Director, author, and Certified Health Coach. She serves as a Weight Loss and Lifestyle Strategist mentoring her clients to improve their health and reach their desired goals.

Chapter 44

Dear Vice President Harris, this poem is for you,

The Color of My Soul

My bells are ringing. My soul is singing.
Praise Song for Madam Vice President, Kamala Harris.

There are colors in the rainbow.
Colors down in the sea
Red orange is the sunset.
But what is the color of my soul?

Blue is a violet.
Blue is the sky.
I see colors in the mountains.
But what is the color of my soul?

We have hang-ups about skin tones.
Hang-ups about each other's hair.
Pandas and zebras are two toned.
Do you really think they care?

Green is the grass
Brown is the earth.
I embrace all colors.
Love is the color of my soul.
Our eyes are many colors.
Brown-eyed, blue-eyed, green.
It's not how they look.
It's what our eyes have seen.

Turquoise is blue green.
Mother-of-pearl is yellowish white.
I embody all colors
Because Love is the color of my soul.
Leopards need their spots.
Tigers need their stripes.
We have to be about Love,
Forget about all the media hype.
Butterflies are multi-colors.
Birds and fish are too.
I am living color
For Love is the color
Of my soul.
Kamala Harris is the USA's
First Woman Vice President.
She is the embodiment of all Colors.
LOVE is the Color she graciously gracefully represents.

Mamma Linda Goss

Mama Linda Goss lives in Baltimore, Maryland, and is an American storyteller and performer in the African diasporic oral tradition. She is a cofounder of the National Association of Black Storytellers, which works to preserve folk traditions.

Chapter 45

Dear Vice President Harris,

Congratulations on being selected by Joe Biden to be his running mate and our first female and minority Vice President of the United States. As a woman and a minority, I am thankful that the leaders of our country are finally recognizing and utilizing the contributions women can bring to the table and to the world.

Your selection by Joe Biden not only broke through that "women need not apply door." It also puts you, a woman, only one or two elections away from the oval office and the presidency.

I am so happy that you are a member of the HBCU family, the Links, AKA, and other sororities or "sistahood" organizations. And to those who say that you are not an African American, I say your father's African ancestors were dragged off the slave ships in Jamaica while my ancestors were on those same ships traveling to the deep south.

Kamala, you are us and we are you. You call yourself a Person of Color; I call myself an African American. We all are the same. You and I are the descendants of a glorious people who came to this continent not by choice but who thrived and excelled nevertheless. You and I rock because we both have that Black Girl Magic!

Congratulations.

Betty Jean Grant

Betty Jean Grant was born in Covington, Tennessee, and relocated to Buffalo, New York. She is a former City Councilmember, Buffalo Board of Education Board member, and a former County Legislator.

Chapter 46

Dear Vice President Harris:

You were always my candidate for multiple reasons but mostly because I saw a woman of color, part African American, part Indian American, who, as Vice President, would work hard for all Americans by returning ethics to the position. I am an African American baby boomer. Ten years ago, I began a path with my father who suffers dementia, prostate cancer, hearing loss, and most recently, a fractured hip. He also tested positive for COVID-19 twice. My father is 100 years old, a WWII veteran, lives in a nursing home and is under hospice care. Please allow me to share a story.

On one of my visits with my father, pre COVID-19, I greeted him with a smile and a vanilla milkshake. Sadness overwhelmed me when he couldn't hold the milkshake. I held it for him, put the straw to his mouth, and he sipped. And when that exhausted him, I fed it to him slowly with a spoon. Afterwards, I fed him his dinner. I wondered if the dementia was progressing. I smiled and occasionally held and kissed his hands. Doing so masked my grief.

I know, as Vice President, you, alongside President Biden, will show leadership that responds to health conditions impacting the elderly and their families. Any threats to Social Security and Medicare would have severe consequences with respect to my father's care.

I am committed to the new administration. Together, we can change four years of apathy.

Sincerely,
Patricia E. Green

Patricia E. Green resides in Littlestown, Pennsylvania, and is a business owner, daughter, wife, mother, and grandmother.

Chapter 47

Dear Vice President, this is a poem for you.

Black Women in Power
I look in the mirror and who do I see?
The image of my mother's strength and courage looking back at me.
But so many only see brown skin, curly hair and full lips
Blunt nose, strong back and generous hips.
They see only the outer me not the person inside
They don't see my faith my passion and my pride.
I'm told I can't be angry at injustice and lower pay
About men trying to control my reproduction without having a say.
Why can't I be angry about Black bodies lying cold in the street
'Bout Lynching and Black children going to bed with nothing to eat.
Why can't I be angry? I'm a Black woman, you see
I'm not allow to be angry without it labeling me.
Take hard times in stride, don't fuss or complain
Be a strong Black woman and bare the problems and pain
Holding down family and job, is it a blessing or curse?
I'll guess I'll finally know when I'm hauled away in the hearse
They wanted to lock Hilary up for exposing secure emails
But no one called her a whore that's reserved for Black females

Black women spent a lifetime contributing to History
Why they hate us so much is not really a mystery.
We intimidate white women and scare the hell out of white men
You know it's the truth so don't try to pretend.
In politics, well you know, we don't really belong
A Black woman in power, now that's all kinds of wrong.
They say we're intellectually inferior, ugly to boot,
Loose morals and poor judgement, now ain't that a hoot.

Aminatu, Nefertiti, Mekeda ruled kingdoms and lead campaigns
That's the African heritage that flows through my veins.
African Queens reigned with power and bravery
Less you forget, my history did not begin with slavery.
Shirley Chisolm, Barbara Jordan and Maxine Waters
Your Grandmothers, Mothers, Aunties and Daughters.
Harvard graduate and First Lady Michelle Obama called a gorilla in heels
I have some names for that white woman so she'll know how it feels
Michelle said go high when they go low
But I can't promise you that, if you call me a ho.'
Removing the earrings and I've got Vaseline
So, you'd better start running before I truly get mean.
Verda Welcome, Carol Moseley Braun, Patricia Roberts Harris
Making Good Trouble, not trying to embarrass.
We're taking off the gloves it's no holds barred
Not settling for the inch, we're demanding the whole damn yard.
Keesha Lance Bottoms, Gwen Moore and Cynthia McKinney
Sheila Jackson Lee, Condoleezza Rice, there are so many
Senators, Representatives, Governors and Mayors from sea to shining sea
Black women in politics who look just like me.
No more back rooms or leftovers it's our time at center stage
Prepare the History books to add a brand-new page.
Sick and tired of being sick and tired, not taking any more
Claiming it now, Kamala Harris for President in 2024.

Sincerely,
Janice Curtis Greene

Janice Curtis Greene lives in Windsor Mill, Maryland. She is President of the National Association of Black Storytellers and serves as a governor-appointed Commissioner on the Maryland Commission of African American History and Culture.

Chapter 48

Dear Vice President Harris:

Congratulations on being: "Simply, Enough!"

You have been chosen as the Vice President for this great country, the United States of America. Suddenly, though, all your previous accomplishments seem to be forgotten and your identity, like that of our former president, Barack Obama, is called into question. Some of those questions, when not asked explicitly, are implied. You must find some of them annoying, if not laughable:

Are you black enough?

Are you Indian enough?

Are you Jamaican enough?

And, are you even American enough to be eligible for this office?

My "Jamaican Sister," look in the mirror every morning and reassure yourself: "Yes, I am Enough!" Like Esther in the Bible, you are called "for such a time as this."

Racial ambiguity and others' inability to fit you into an ethnic box is not your problem. Those who have a problem with the dynamics of your ethnicity have to settle that problem within themselves. You have issues of far greater importance to capture your attention and on which to focus, such as finding creative ways to help a divided nation heal. America today needs Kamala. We need to show the world that a black girl or a brown girl can take her rightful place among the brightest and best because she is one of the brightest and best.

Our stories might be different but our struggles to prove that we are good enough have some common threads. Born on the sandy shores of Negril, Jamaica, to poor parents, I have never outgrown having to prove that I am good enough. I rose to the top of my career in State Government; I wrote and published my first book, *Warm Regards: Inspiration 365*; I served my countries of birth and adoption and, I consistently serve the communities in which I have worked and lived. Still, it seems that I still have to prove to some that I am good enough.

You are good enough and "simply enough" Kamala, so here's a word of encouragement from scripture for the journey ahead: "Have I not commanded you? Be strong and of good courage; do not be afraid, nor be dismayed, for the Lord your God is with you wherever you go." Joshua 1:9.

You are more than "good enough" for the position of Vice President of the United States of America. You are "Simply, Enough!"

Warm Regards,
Elvie Guthrie-Lewis

Elvie Guthrie-Lewis lives in Mississippi and is an author, a motivational speaker, a Registered Dietitian, a Certified Public Manager, a writer, and a storyteller.

Chapter 49

Dear Vice President Harris:

I am writing in enthusiastic support of your election as Vice President of the United States. Your exciting win empowers us all to be better citizens and to enhance our efforts to serve our country, especially our country's youth. That has long been a passion of mine. Of special interest for me and my colleagues at the Home of Champions is a program that identifies leaders among foster care youth as well as provides the support necessary for them to achieve their full potential as strong role models and productive members of society. For instance, 18%–24% of college-age foster youth are enrolled in college in New York State, but only 3% graduate. This is an unforgivable statistic and points to their need for additional support in special programs such as mentoring and a full range of activities to cultivate their careers. More important than one single program, the country needs additional programs emphasizing youth who have transitioned out of foster care and have been accepted into college on their own merit. This is a group in which there has been little or no interest. But I know that you are concerned deeply about young people who are so close to achieving some of their dreams, and they just need another "push" at the right time and place.

Vice President Kamala, it seems that the whole world is excited about you in this new important position. And, in your new job as Vice President, I urge you to reach out broadly to embrace those foster care students who are "aging out" of foster care service but who still need a governmental mechanism to encourage partnerships among colleges and social service organizations and unique programs, like Home of Champions, that provide other needed services. These partnerships will ensure that our young people in foster care will have access to the opportunities, resources, and mentoring necessary for them to successfully cultivate their careers. We do not want to see foster care children fall between the cracks or falter because we have not fully met their needs.

Again, we look at you for support of the many children in foster care who are striving to move forward. They are depending on you, Mrs. Vice President.

Sincerely,
Judith Halbreich

Judith Halbreich lives in Buffalo, New York, and is Director of the Home of Champions.

Chapter 50

Dear Vice President Harris:

My family celebrated the night you were announced as Joe Biden's running mate. In fact, we deemed dinner that night, "Crab Legs for Kamala." Not only did I celebrate, but I also let out a long sigh in anticipation of what was to come. Obviously, we acknowledge how historic this moment is. But, as a black woman in leadership, I know all that you will endure and all you must have already endured to have ascended as high as you already have in your career. For only a sister knows what a sister goes through.

Thank you for every morning you will wake up with a headache and sore shoulders from the stress of the weight you carry as the barrier of the label "first." Thank you for blazing the trail so bright for every little girl who is climbing the mountain behind you. Thank you, Kamala.

Know that we stand with you and strive for greatness in order to match your greatness.

Best,
Alexandria Harris

Alexandria Harris, Esq., lives in Newark, New Jersey, and is Executive Director of The Andrew Goodman Foundation.

Chapter 51

Hello Vice President Kamela Harris:

I hope my letter finds you well. As VP you will undoubtedly inherit countless issues and concerns to be addressed that affects millions of Americans. One issue that is near and dear to my heart affects the most vulnerable among us, our children and child safety, particularly as it relates to custody and custodial access.

Like you, I am a mother who is a strong and positive presence in her children's lives. All of my children are now grown. Yet, at 58 yrs of age, I am parenting, nurturing, educating, protecting, advocating for, raising, and stabilizing an extraordinary grandchild.

There are tens of thousands of us grandparents, and the numbers are growing, who are parenting grandchildren. What laws can support grandparents and even great-grandparents in their efforts to care for children? How can the federal government acknowledge and provide financial and respite relief for this specific population? Also, how do we effectively protect children and keep them safe in lieu of custodial access?

Moreover, the government has a duty to pass laws and policies for the stewards of the state and the courts to implement to help protect children and support caregivers particularly us grandparents. I am steadfastly advocating for my grandson yet there are far too many children who are left in horrific situations by the courts and the stewards of the state until the unthinkable happens.

In closing, why is the United States of America guilty of not effectively protecting children? And where are the hundreds of children unlawfully taken from their parents at our borders and are now missing?!! We as a country have to do better by our future leaders, our children. Thank you for your time.

Warm regards,
Janice Lovon Harris

Janice Lovon Harris is a Disabled Army Veteran living in Baltimore, Maryland. She is a mother of four and grandmother to six children.

Chapter 52

Dear Vice President Harris,

I'm often reminded of an old gospel song that says, "May the works I've done speak for me. May the service I give, speak for me. When I'm resting in my grave, and there's nothing to be said, May the works I've done and the service I gave, speak for me." This song resonates with me and I hope with you as well. I truly believe the song speaks to the work you've done for many years in ensuring equality for all. You are quoted as saying that your "amma" would say, "Don't sit around and complain about things. Do something." Well, Vice President Harris, you are "doing something." You have made your "amma" proud. Just like you, my mother passed from colon cancer. And just like you, it is my goal to always make her proud.

Your "amma" is proud of how you have united people. You have united individuals and you believe that "our unity is our strength and our diversity is our power." We reject the myth of "us" vs. "them." We are in this together. Your "amma" is proud of how you have fought against injustices. You have fought for children and survivors of sexual assault. You have fought against transnational gangs. And you've taken on the biggest banks and helped take down one of the biggest for-profit colleges. Your "amma" is proud of your stance on abortion. You believe that we cannot tolerate a perspective that is about going backward and not understanding that women have agency. Women have value. Women have authority to make decisions about their own lives and their own bodies.

Your "amma" is proud of your stance on the protests of 2020. You've said, "Let's speak the truth: people are protesting because Black people have been treated as less than human in America. Because our country has never fully addressed the systemic racism that has plagued our country since its earliest days, it is the duty of every American to fix it. No longer can some wait on the sidelines, hoping for incremental change. In times like this, silence is complicity."

My prayer for you is that the Lord continues to bless you with the strength, patience, and tenacity to continue serving our country and making it even better and equal for all.

I encourage you to continue to stand in and speak your truth, even when you may have to stand alone . . . so that your works and service will continue to speak for you. Not only is your "amma" proud of you, many women across the world are proud of you!

Stay Blessed.

Nina S. Heard, MBA

Nina Heard lives in Buffalo, New York and is Cofounder of Friends for A Better Buffalo.

Chapter 53

Dear Madam Vice President:

Though we are in the midst of turbulent times, when I saw you on the campaign trail, I saw hope. Hope for me as a child of civil rights activists who have been forced to watch the next generation fight the same old fight against hate. Hope for me as the mother of a young son who might conceivably only learn about such hate in the context of a classroom. Hope as an American that we can and will do and be better as a society.

I had the opportunity to write postcards to registered democrats in my area, encouraging them to make their plan to vote immediately. I rotated through my various reasons for voting, some of which include needing a better and more cohesive national response to the COVID-19 crisis, wanting to see criminal justice reform, longing for a hopeful future and a return to decency. You represent all of that and so much more. I could not wait to pridefully cast my ballot. You are truly our ancestors' wildest dreams come true. I wish you health and wellness, and I hope that you find moments of Zen amidst the chaos.

With love and gratitude,
Alison Higgins

Alison Higgins was born and raised in Philadelphia, Pennsylvania, and now resides in Montgomery County, Pennsylvania. She is a mother, wife, daughter, sister, friend, and voter.

Chapter 54

Dear Vice President "Kamala":

I love the sound of your name. It's soothing, melodic and reminds me of "jump rope rhymes" of my youth when little Black girls got together to play with clothesline rope on broken sidewalks. Although it was fun and play it was the beginning of a sisterhood bond that strengthened over the years.

Kamala, Kamala
Turn all around
Kamala, Kamala
Touch the ground
Kamala, Kamala
Go upstairs
Kamala, Kamala
Say your prayers
Kamala, Kamala
What you say
Vice President
Of the USA.

The journey that you are embarking upon will usher applause and spew venom often in the same space. However, be encouraged. Hold your head up high. Break the ceiling and touch the sky. We'll see you on Black Lives Plaza in 2021.

Blessings,
Sharon Jordan Holley

Sharon Jordan Holley is a retired Librarian, black bookstore owner, and a world-renowned storyteller, and she lives in Buffalo, New York.

Chapter 55

Dear Vice President "Kamala":

August 2020 brought the historic moment of a Black woman being named the Vice-Presidential nominee for the Democratic Party in advance of the 2020 election. Women of all races have fought and died for the right to participate in the national political processes. Joe Biden's panel of possible candidates for this vice-presidential position revealed that he was inspired to nominate women from different regions, races, and experiences. Kamala Harris, chosen with her unwavering commitment to fairness and equity, emerged as our North Star, lighting the way to social justice.

Personally, from my position I experienced a rush of excitement when (finally) a major party nominated a woman of color to a major seat on the Presidential ticket. With 50+ years on this planet, I am so accustomed to anyone who looks like me being silenced and sidelined. Senator Harris's inclusion created a distinctive yet overdue presence in executive presidential politics. The new direction in American politics ignited an exuberance in populations that are typically ignored or forgotten. Students, alumni, faculty, and staff from HBCUs (Historical Black Colleges and Universities) swelled with pride that an HBCU graduate from Howard University was poised to join the nation's executive branch.

Clearly, after the Democratic presidential debates where Senator Harris truthfully told her then-competitor Joe Biden about her experiences with school busing, the world saw that Harris is a fighter. As a prosecutor and advocate, she knows how to stand her ground with poise. With her election as Vice President, she will need those skills more than ever. Her savvy in managing conflict will always be needed as a sword and shield.

Like any woman of color in the spotlight, Kamala Harris was and will be met with countless tyrants, bullies, and scoundrels. Not even seven days after her nomination, she was hit with racist/sexist markers such as being "angry," and "the meanest, most horrible, disrespectful senator." In our not too distant memory, Michelle Obama was the target of trolling in the media during her husband's first campaign. Georgia gubernatorial candidate Stacy Abrams spoke out about a racist robocall sent to constituents during her campaign to suppress voter participation. The robocall stated, "This is the magical negro, Oprah Winfrey, asking you to make my fellow negress, Stacey Abrams, the governor of Georgia."

Women of color in politics have been the constant targets of racist and sexist statements through cyber abuse, bullying, and mobbing. For example, the President led the verbal attacks against four progressive women of color wwere elected to Congress: Representatives Ilhan Omar of Minnesota, Alexandria Ocasio-Cortez of New York, Rashida Tlaib of Michigan, and Ayanna Pressley of Massachusetts. Trump claimed that these women were not American and should return to their homes overseas. Senior Congresswoman from California, Maxine Waters also has been the target of aggressive and racist death threats. In the summer of 2018, Stephen Taubert, a 61-year-old white male, launched racist death threats at both Congresswoman Waters and former president Barack Obama. For his terroristic threats, Taubert, who also called the Capitol Police Officer a "N----r Boy" over 30 times in an interview, was sentenced to four years in prison.

Events during the summer of 2020 illustrate that such racist and sexist behavior does not only emerge from the public at large. One's own colleagues construct pathways of incivility and disrespect. Ted Yoho, Republican congressman from Florida, called Alexandria Ocasio-Cortez a "F--king B---ch" while coming down the capital stairs. After Yoho misrepresented his character assassination of Ocasio-Cortez to the press, Congresswoman Ocasio-Cortez poignantly took the Congress floor the next day to give the following statement:

"What I do have an issue with is using women, our wives, our daughters as shields and excuses for poor behavior. Mr. Yoho mentioned that he has a wife and two daughters. I am two years younger than Mr. Yoho's youngest daughter. I am someone's daughter, too. My father, thankfully, is not alive to see how Mr. Yoho treated his daughter. My mother got to see Mr. Yoho's disrespect on the floor of this House towards me on television. And I am here because I have to show my parents that I am their daughter and that they did not raise me to accept abuse from men. What Mr. Yoho did was give permission for men to use that language against his daughters. Having a daughter does not make a man decent. Having a wife does not make a decent man. Treating people with dignity and respect makes a decent man. This kind of language is not new. I have tossed men out of bars that have used language like Mr. Yoho's . . . This is not new, and that is the problem."

As a familiar cliché notes, past behavior predicts future performance. The performance of too many people in reaction to women of color in politics has exuded incredibly violent and disrespectful behavior. These instances not only disparage the women in the aforementioned scenarios, these examples chronicle a lapse in humanitarian behavior for those who perpetrate such aggression and incivility. One may ponder, "What part brings this vitriolic hatred, the race, the gender, the age?" These women politicians are at the intersections of a diversity of demographic markers and remain in the crosshairs of constant incivility. Perhaps the bullies and trolls motivated by hateful xenophobia do not recognize that while these women have proven they are resilient enough to withstand such attacks, the damaging language erodes the general civility in our communities.

I could continue with other women of color in various sectors, such as Venus Williams, Megan Markle, Leslie Jones, who have endured and continue to deal with racist and misogynist hostility in the press. Though I have every confidence that Vice President Harris will continue with the same poise and determination that she exuded in this campaign season, I see that she, like most women of color, will need to transcend this tremendous gulf of bullying behaviors and racist/sexist slurs to emerge victorious on the other side. In this context, as this North Star lights her own way to 1600 Pennsylvania Avenue, we women of color are fortified by this light in our own respective struggles for equity and fairness in our own communities.

Sincerely,
Leah P. Hollis

Leah P. Hollis, EdD, is Associate Professor, Department of Advanced Studies, Leadership & Policy at Morgan State University, Baltimore, Maryland.

Chapter 56

Dear Vice President Harris:

"Many daughters have done noble things, but you surpass them all . . . "

Proverbs 31:29 (Berean version)

Today you carry forth the hopes and dreams of women and girls of color beautifully, and with enormous poise, grace, and a determination so fierce and unapologetic that surely the ancestors stand and rejoice. The pride that our generations around the world feel is reflected in their faces and hearts, for they proudly see in your bold stride a gait of their own.

The brilliance and joy that emanates from your eyes gently reminds us that through sacrifice and perseverance, Harriet, Sojourner, Fannie Lou, Shirley, Barbara, Shyamala, and Rajam don't just live on in us, they push us forward and insist that we soar with our own wings and sing our own songs. They poignantly remind us that this is our time, our opportunity to matter, our right to bask in every sacrifice and dream that allowed this day to finally dawn.

You were created for such a time as this, and as you prepare for what comes next, please know that we who believe in freedom will not rest until it comes. The road ahead will be rough, but we have faced long, rocky roads and adversity before, but we laughed, kept stepping, and refused to swallow our own briny tears.

Many of our grandmothers and sisters died with their songs wound tightly inside them, yearning to be sung triumphantly, but they were hellbent on humming, watching, and believing until this day arrived. As you step forth and take your rightful place in history, remember power is heavy armor—use it wisely and with noble purpose when you must and make a mighty blow. A clear conscience and a sound mind are to be cherished, admired, and carefully guarded, for in them are your strength and ultimate authority.

Go now with our Creator who has plans "to prosper you and give you hope and a future." May your steps be ordered by God and your faith refreshed like the morning dew. Jeremiah 29:11

Sincerely,
Cynthia A. Bond Hopson

Cynthia A. Bond Hopson, PhD, is an educator and best-selling author who lives in Cordova, Tennessee, with her husband, Roger, a United Methodist minister.

Chapter 57

Dear Vice President Harris:

I will pray for you every day, wishing for you a double portion of strength, wisdom, understanding, and patience, as you prepare yourself for your purposeful assignment as Vice President of The United States of America.

Vice President Kamala, praying has given me hope in my life, as a woman of color with a hand amputee visible disability. I pray for strength, wisdom, understanding, and patience every day to combat the insults of an ableism society mindset.

So, as you go on your purposeful assignment, please remember that you are not alone as you step into your VICTORY!!!

Sincerely,
Cheryl "Uncut Diamond" Hubbard

Cheryl "Uncut Diamond" Hubbard lives in New Jersey and is owner of a food company specializing in nuts and dried fruits.

Chapter 58

Dear Vice President Harris:

Thank you. I wanted to say that since you stepped on the political scene representing the State of California, African Americans, Asian Americans, Alpha Kappa Alpha Sorority Inc., Historically Black Colleges and Universities, and everyone else that you have sworn to advocate and defend are excited. Your very presence is an inspiration and a threat. You inspire anyone that can see a piece of themselves in you, but you also threaten any force that is against accountability and progress. As my Soror, I pray that every good and perfect thing is presented to you as a resource to better the democracy in which we live. I pray for God's perfect peace when difficult decisions are made and answers are required. I pray for discernment for the greater good and a remembrance to all that has created you. Take your place, defend justice, protect the people, love God, and be kind to yourself.

Sisterly,
Candacé M. Jackson

Candacé M. Jackson, JD, is alumna of Hampton University and SUNY Buffalo Law School. She resides in Washington, DC, where she works in the coaching, legal, creative, and education industries.

Chapter 59

Dear Vice President Harris,

What an opportunity to achieve the political ambition of many politically inclined American women! When your historic campaign bid in 2019 for the Democratic presidential nomination in a super-saturated field ended, most of us thought the opportunity would remain dormant for another four more years. However, in 2020 the synergy of the dual anniversaries of the Sesquicentennial of the 15th amendment in February and the centennial of the 19th amendment in August provided a perfect backdrop for another outcome. You were nominated as the 2020 Vice Presidential candidate for the Democratic Party—the first woman of color in the nation's 244 years of history! And, now you are Vice President. Amazing, inspiring, challenging, daunting, and historical all in one moment of time, but in fact your meteoric success is built upon the bodies, dreams, and agency of earlier Black American women politicians, clubwomen, church women, and concerned citizens. You know this and cited this fact in your acceptance speech—that was affirming and in the tradition of your triple otherness–an African American, HBCU graduate, and sorority woman.

As a historian I would like to share insight about two political foremothers who too were both HBCU grads, sorority women, and political firsts occupying office during turbulent times. Their legacies opened potentialities for others who occupied the margins of society—not because of deficiency but because of de facto relegation because of race and gender. Nevertheless, they did not let that stop them—in fact it impelled them to declare their candidacies and campaigns, eventually getting elected to their offices. The two women are Verda F. Welcome and Victorine Q. Adams. Mrs. Welcome served as the first African American woman elected to the State Senate. She represented Maryland. Mrs. Adams was the first African American woman elected to the

Baltimore City Council. Contemporaries and residents of Baltimore, these two women worked in concert with their various circles including Morgan State University, Sigma Gamma Rho and Delta Sigma Theta, and church and political groups they created. It is my desire to inspire you to know a scintilla of the cavalcade of Black women from Maryland who threw up paths in the wilderness of American politics for such a time as this in the 21st century.

Verda Freeman Welcome (March 18, 1907–April 22, 1990) credited her mother as the person who taught her how "to carry myself as a woman" and that being an African American and a woman were not barriers. She began her career as a teacher, where she observed the impact injustice, discrimination, and inequality had on African American children from poor building conditions to lack of school supplies. In 1939, she obtained a Bachelor of Science degree from Morgan State College and later joined Delta Sigma Theta sorority.

Her advocacy for the children and larger lack of city services through Black neighborhoods morphed into politics, where she could exercise her passionate concern for bettering and advocating for the African American community. Her first elected office was to a neighborhood group, the Northwest Improvement Association, in 1946; through the NIA she targeted overcrowded buildings, poor sanitation, crime, racism, and poor medical facilities. Her advocacy wrought change and increased her visibility. In 1958, she campaigned for Baltimore's Fourth District State Delegate seat in Maryland. After winning the election, Verda Freeman Welcome vowed to represent all the people in her district and alleviate racial and class divisions. Her record promoted gun and smoking laws, public accommodations for the blind, legalizing interracial marriages, and ending welfare recipient harassment. In 1959, at the age of 52, Welcome won a seat in the Maryland House of Delegates, Fourth District. As a Delegate, Welcome pushed for civil rights reform in public accommodations, equal protection under the law, and mail-in voter registration. In 1962, she challenged the "old boys' political machine" for the State Senate, campaigning with a platform directed at inclusion and representing all the people. She won! Senator Welcome served the state of Maryland from 1962 to 1982. Her legacy of leadership, mentoring, and advocacy removed literal and figurative barriers for all Marylanders seeking to live in a fair and equitable society. She, due to her numerous achievements, was inducted into the Maryland Women's Hall of Fame in 1988.

Victorine Quille Adams (April 28, 1912–January 8, 2006) attended Robert Brown Elliot School #104, Frederick Douglass High School, and Coppin Normal school—all public institutions that were segregated schools created for "colored" people. In June 1940, Victorine graduated summa cum laude from Morgan State College with a Bachelor of Science degree in education and later joined Sigma Gamma Rho sorority. She worked as a school teacher from 1935 until the 1940s.

In 1943, Victorine, along with two teachers, a social worker, and a lawyer, chartered the National Council of Negro Women Baltimore section. Maryland did not ratify the 19th amendment until 1941. Baltimore City judge Oscar Lesser challenged the 19th all the way to the US Supreme Court and lost. Still Maryland did not certify the ratification until February 25, 1958. Toward this end, in 1946 she founded the Colored Women's Democratic Campaign Committee. The CWDCC's motto "if democracy is worth fighting for its worth voting for." Their initiative welcomed all, registered all, and enlightened all interested in placing more women in politics. Their first campaign resulted in the election of Harry A. Cole to Maryland State Senate. Judge Cole was the first African American elected State Senator in Maryland, a Morgan State College graduate and member of Alpha Phi Alpha fraternity. They also mobilized support for Verda F. Welcome resulting in her being the first African American woman elected to the Maryland Senate in 1962.

On August 19, 1958 she cofounded Woman Power, incorporated with Mrs. Ethel P. Rich. Their three aims were to mobilize Black women for political action/power, community involvement, and educational commitment. Woman Power's motto was "each one, reach one, each one, teach one." They believed that every woman could teach something and every woman could learn something. Men were welcome to join the Minute Men, an affiliate of the Woman Power.

In 1966 she successfully ran for the Maryland House of Delegates, but resigned after a year and won a seat on the Baltimore City Council.

She realized that the city needed to have a compassionate ear and voice in city government. Her legacy was mentoring and crusading for the voiceless in the city. Senator Barbara Mikulski stated at Victorine's funeral: "I learned [from Adams] about how to get things done. You really did change Baltimore. You really did change the world."

Victorine served 4 terms from 1967 to 1983. Her tenure on the City Council inaugurated the continuous presence of African American women in Baltimore city politics. She was inducted to the Maryland Women's Hall of Fame in 2020.

Both Verda and Victorine were members of the National Council of Negro Women, founded in 1935 by Mary McLeod Bethune. They adopted four purposes for its organization: to unite national member organizations in a NCNW; to educate, encourage and effect the participation of Negro women in civic, political, economic and educational activities and institutions; to serve as a clearing house for the dissemination of activities concerning women; and to plan, initiate, and carry out projects that develop, benefit, and integrate the Negro and the nation. These women were wives, sorority members, church workers, professionals, and politically conscious citizens whose numbers nudged a space at the table. These women brought ideas of equality, fairness, and humanity for all citizens regardless of race, color, or creed. Through the NCNW's national network and coordinated efforts, the days of Jim Crow, black women's invisibility, and the silence of poor urban minority populations were numbered. This is our tradition as Black women in America. Our means may differ however the desired end is the same: a clean environment, safe communities, and equitable life for all Americans.

In closing, during those quiet moments of contemplation, weighing decisions of importance, or fully engaging mistruths, consider the lives of Verda Welcome and Victorine Adams. Both women, born over 100 years ago, lived through an era of vicious racial violence, gender indifference, and de facto discrimination—and yet they exercised such persistent courage. Moreover, they were touched by the life and words of Mary McLeod Bethune, who stated, "If I have a legacy to leave my people, it is my philosophy of living and serving. I pray now that my philosophy may be helpful to those who share my vision of a world of Peace, Progress, Brotherhood, and Love."

God bless your historic journey and future with grace, wisdom, understanding, and knowing that the sisterhood of African Americans are here on earth and in heaven cheering you on!

Sincerely,
Ida E. Jones

Ida E. Jones, PhD, currently lives in Washington, DC. She is the first University Archivist hired at Morgan State University and is the author of four books.

Chapter 60

Dear Vice President Harris:

I am very honored to send you this letter to tell you how much I am with you, and how much I have been following your career, your achievements, and what you are doing right now. I am also honored because you are a woman educated in the Law, and you are a woman of conviction who has always fought for the well-being of the American population. You are a role model. We thank Mr. Joe Biden for choosing such a great woman. I don't believe that there was another option. Here in the Ivory Coast we are all convinced that you and Joe Biden will form a great team and bring the best to the Americans and the rest of the world.

On the whole of the African continent, the support was for the Biden-Kamala duo. We were ready and the entire world waited with us for the good result of this election. God almighty will be with you and will guide you in this wonderful journey.

Respectfully,
Hubertine Kassi-Adjoussou

Hubertine Kassi-Adjoussou is an Ivorian lawyer in the capital city of Abidjan and is a member of the Bar Association of the Ivory Coast. She is very much interested in children's rights and works closely with an orphanage in one of the districts of the city.

Chapter 61

Dear Vice President Harris:

I am sending out congratulations to you with an energized heart and joyful spirit. We may never meet, but as a woman/black, an immigrant/Jamaican, and a single working mother I want to wish you the utmost success, blessings, and guidance in your new position as VP. I have watched your performances over the years—you have such compassion, strength, and vigor, and I know in my heart that Vice President Biden has made the right decision and that you will do an excellent job serving the USA as Vice President.

The attacks are coming, I see them, but that's what cowards do. However, your love and genuine compassion for our country and its people will prevail. Continue to stand tall, keep the faith, and never back down. We the women of this country stand behind you all the way.

"Go Get 'Em, Kam."

Sincerely yours,
Nadine Khan

Nadine Khan is a nurse, Jamaican immigrant, and a single mother of a daughter who is now in college.

Chapter 62

Dear Vice President Harris:

There were no words to encompass all that I felt when you elected to run as the Vice President with Joe Biden. Your presence on the campaign trail gave women of color hope and encouragement that despite all obstacles we may encounter we can and will persevere and thrive. You have given us the motivation to set the bar high for ourselves, achieving all that we dream to accomplish. You have fought the good fight, finished the race, and have kept the faith. As you become our first woman of color Vice President of these United States of America, I pray for your success. God Bless You. Continue to make "GOOD TROUBLE."

With Love, respect, and admiration,
Brenda K. Kinsler

Brenda K. Kinsler is a Senior Consultant at Be Strong Families. She has been a social worker for 32 years and employed at the Philadelphia Department of Human Services for most of that time.

Chapter 63

Dear Vice President Harris,

I am writing this letter to you during a time where I have very little faith in our country. As a middle-aged Black woman, I have been around long enough to see a few things. I have witnessed the explosion of the internet and social media. I remember a time where we weren't bombarded with so much hate and division simply because it wasn't so readily accessible. I find myself attempting social media and news detoxes in the hope that I can reset my mind and heart. I am beginning to feel hatred, and that is not me or who I want to be. I need things to change for me, my children, and everyone who feels outrage on a daily basis.

I know that you will have many letters to peruse where you will be informed of the importance of the role you are playing in creating a bittersweet history for our people. You will be told that you have a monumental task before you. You will be warned that people are depending on you as the country weeps, burns, marches, divides, and dies. I am certain that it is not lost on you how important your task will be. You will be criticized no matter what you do. You will be hated simply because you are a Black woman who is unapologetically powerful. You will be judged by a country that can't seem to progress far enough to realize the contributions that we have made as a people and continue to make every day. We built this country.

Honestly, Kamala, I once knew very little about you as I went about my daily life here in Rochester, New York. I didn't know much about you until I watched you on television one day questioning someone with the masterful precision of a surgeon. I watched you back someone into a corner with their own lies in a way that reminded me of the few times I tried to "run game" on my mother when I was little. I looked at you and thought "she is not the one to be playing with" and "y'all picked the wrong one" as the individual in the hot seat squirmed. You dished out "piping hot accountability," and they were not ready.

This country is not ready for you, Kamala. This country is not ready to have a Black woman who tells it like it is, plays no games, is brilliant, and calls "bullshit" like very few I have ever seen. I believe this country is not ready to let go of its preconceived notions of who you are as a Black and Indian woman. This country prefers to put people in manageable stereotypic boxes to maintain their own sense of comfort, justify their hatred, and refuse change.

A certain individual, who shall remain unnamed as he is not worth the text, called you a "ho" a while ago. This person has been spewing lies about people for years while maintaining a hypocritical lifestyle that would lead a true human being to feel shame. He called you a "ho" because attacking you as a woman is low-hanging fruit. He wanted to support the "Angry Black Woman" narrative. I was pissed for you when I heard that shit. Then I paused. I looked past this juvenile provocation and thought about the word "ho" and how I might reclaim it in my mind. The result is "Honesty Operative." That is who you are to me. Words have been created since the beginning of time, and they only have the power that we give them.

Black women have been called all types of names throughout history in an effort to strip us of our humanity, sexualize us, belittle us, trivialize our accomplishments and "test" us to the max. That's ok, though. I chose to call you Vice President Harris . . . the Honesty Operative.

Give 'em hell as the new Vice President! I am with you.

Respectfully,
Darci Lane-Williams

Darci Lane-Williams teaches at the University of Rochester, New York, where she lives with her husband and children.

Chapter 64

Dear Vice President!

You have made history—you have shown the world that the power of women is woven into the fabric of all that is good and right and possible. You stand on the shoulders of great foremothers—Harriet Tubman, Ida B. Wells-Barnett, Alice Paul, Margaret Chase Smith, Fannie Lou Hamer, Ella Baker, Kalpana Chawla, Hillary Clinton, and countless more who forged a path to freedom, equality, justice and self-determination. That path has often been blocked by forces determined to keep superiority for a few and subordination for the rest. But, like you, those women refused to be bound by the chains of sexism, racism, and elitism, and proved powerful in their resolve to confront those who sought to deny them. Let those women—let all of us—be your bridge that carries you over to the White House, a bridge to fulfilling the promise of America.

Thank you for your leadership and all you have done. Thank you for being the fresh new face of inspiration for girls and women everywhere, and I, we, cannot wait to call you Vice President Kamala Harris in 2021.

With great affection and excitement,
Kate Clifford Larson

Kate Clifford Larson, PhD, lives in Vermont and is a historian and author of *Bound for the Promised Land: Harriet Tubman, Portrait of an American Hero* and *Walk With Me: A Biography of Fannie Lou Hamer.*

Chapter 65

Dear Vice President Harris,

Greetings Dear Sister Queen Kamala,

Welcome to your destiny!

I believe your journey was charted by the alignment of stars on the day you were born. Your DNA is rich with compassion and determination, reflecting your birth into a family of generational activists committed to civil rights and a quest to advance global understanding among all people. Your life trajectory was clear, even though you may not have understood at such a young age. It was because of the courage of your parents and grandparents.

I wonder, did you hear the lilting voice of your mother, encouraging you, praising you for your relentless pursuit in the cause of justice for the most vulnerable among us? Standing on the shore of the Indian Ocean, as you scattered her ashes, I believe she sang to you in the beautiful voice of the young girl from Tamil Nadur who was adored for her gift of singing. She sang of her love for you and her deep pride that you have donned the family mantle, the familial tradition of urging a reexamination of values in our Republic. As a woman whose formative years were filled with engagement and interactions among diverse cultures and perspectives on heritage; your life is a composite of scholarship, science, creativity, activism, and a worldview that is broad and open and embracing of the change that is critically needed at this time.

I am among the thousands, the hundreds of thousands, who support your effort to bring renewed faith in our leadership and our government. I am among the many who pledge to stand by you as you make your sojourn along a path littered with landmines planted by opponents and their unwavering assault on your life and character that only serves to define their own vulgarity and self-interests rooted in ignorance, greed, power mongering, and desire to advance their oligarchy.

Success and achievement are no strangers to you; neither is controversy nor disappointment, and, like all of us, pain, joy, anger and jubilation have all found a permanent place in our hearts. But we know and understand there is no room for defeat. We understand there is no room for capitulation to circumstances that undermine efforts to rectify injustices, undermine efforts to bring about economic parity, or challenge the right of all citizens to be safe in their homes, walking their dogs, playing in the park, eating in restaurants, or exercising their First Amendment Rights to demand our government take action against any and all parties who threaten the individual safety of American citizens.

Vice President Harris, you are standing at the threshold of political change that will resonate across continents, awaken dreams seeded in the field of infinite possibilities, and reignite hope in the hearts of many where hope has flickered and dimmed. It will not be easy. But you have walked across a bed of nails, burning coals, and searing criticism and survived. I believe you have the heart of a lion, the soul of a warrior, and the love of your ancestors to hold you up. We, in the village of your supporters, will be there with them. You are now indelibly printed on the pages of history; stand tall, be strong, we are counting on you.

Peace and blessings,
Celeste M. Lawson

Celeste M. Lawson lives in Buffalo, New York, and is a well-known local artist. She is also a poet and an art advocate.

Chapter 66

Dear Vice President Harris;

Watching all the goings-on in the US these days, with all the mess, darkness, hatred, and vitriol, your election as VP is one incredibly bright light amidst America's bleakness and I want to encourage you to continue to fight—if for nothing else, to fight for my kids. Seeing another brilliant, beautiful, and strong black woman on the political scene makes my heart sing, especially seeing the impact you have on white males, and I look forward to the great things you and Biden will do in the White House, and four years later, when all my friends anticipate you will be sworn in as POTUS.

I abandoned the US in 2017 and am living a most marvelous life in Madagascar. My two grown children still live in Oakland, CA, and though I hope to convince them to follow my lead and leave the States, for now, anyways, they are committed to remaining there. Though I don't believe the US was ever "great" for people of color, I am encouraged what your candidacy means to those of us who grew up during Jim Crow, the Vietnam War, and the Civil Rights struggle, fighting the good fight. I've thrown in the towel, exited stage left, but seeing your poise, your careful thought, your refusal to back down gives me hope that somehow things can actually change for the better in the US.

I wish you nothing but success and look forward to watching you continue to rise. You are truly a force for good in the Universe.

Respectfully,
Lisa B. Lee

Lisa B. Lee is a retired computer nerd and lives in Mahajanga, Madagascar, Africa.

Chapter 67

Dear Vice President Harris:

I am honored to write this letter to you in support of your work as a leading light in the United States Senate and as the new Vice President of the United States. Congratulations on your selection by Joe Biden to join the Democratic ticket! This is an awesome responsibility that you have undertaken. I applaud Joe Biden's foresight in selecting you and your willingness to assume the mantle.

I am writing this letter to you as I grieve the recent passing of my beloved Mother. Mother passed away in May of this year after a long battle with dementia. My mother was a superstar academician at the University of Pittsburgh in the Africana Studies Department for 37 years. She was an activist and she founded and served as Artistic Director of the Kuntu Repertory Theatre at the University of Pittsburgh. Like your Mother, she was a trailblazer and an amazing role model and mentor for my sister and me. I know that she would have been delighted to know that you ran on the Biden/Harris ticket! She pledged Delta Sigma Theta Sorority Inc. at Dillard University in 1951. Mother began her career in Houston as a Speech and Drama teacher in segregated public schools in violation of Brown vs. Board of Education of Topeka. After teaching in Houston for 19 years, she attended Carnegie Mellon University and earned a doctorate in English prior to joining the faculty at Pitt. She is with my Father and the Ancestors now.

I am standing on her shoulders and determined to do my part to make this country and the world a better place. I hope my Mother's story inspires you, for you are standing on her shoulders also, as you have embarked on this path of higher office and meeting and handling the challenges of political partisanship, intense and often unfair scrutiny of every detail of your life, conspiracy theories, misinformation, disinformation, and gamesmanship.

So, I also write to you from the vantage point of grief about the lack of opportunity, lack of equity, and the public health crisis and social justice issues that confront us every day. I began my legal career as a Law Clerk to a Federal Judge in Philadelphia. I then moved to DC to serve as a Trial Lawyer in the US Department of Justice, Civil Rights Division, during the Carter Administration. I was assigned to the Voting Rights Section. I was a trial team member in voting rights cases in Alabama and Mississippi. I also served as a DOJ Observer in elections all over the South, pursuant to Section 5 of the Voting Rights Act.

It has been tough for me to watch the various efforts at voter suppression and challenges to the integrity of our system of voting. Although the attacks on our democratic system and democratic norms are a source of grieving, I still have so much hope in the future of our country and the future of our democracy. Your professionalism and your uniquely American story are a great source of pride and hope for me. Your education, integrity, history of public service and devotion to family all add up to you being the right person at the right time to make this historic leap into higher office.

I have met you and heard you speak many times. I welcomed you to Comcast Corporation Headquarters in Philadelphia for a fundraiser. I have attended fundraisers for you at Paula Madison's beautiful home in Martha's Vineyard, and my husband and I attended the family brunch fundraiser at your sister and brother-in-law's home in Martha's Vineyard in 2019 during your presidential campaign. I served as a Board Member at Howard University for 12 years, and I sat on the stage with you when you received an honorary degree and delivered the commencement address. So, I have had an opportunity to personally observe you from afar and in real time. You clearly have the intelligence, integrity, confidence, compassion, humanity, trial lawyer skills, and emotional intelligence that will result in your being the best Vice President ever! And it goes without saying that you could be the best President ever! As a member of Delta Sigma Theta Sorority Inc. and the niece of an AKA, I am thrilled to see how members of the Divine Nine and other sororities and fraternities are saying your name out loud and volunteered their time and treasure to ensure that the Biden /Harris ticket emerged victorious on November 3rd.

In my career in the Justice Department, the City of Philadelphia, as a partner in an Am Law 200 law firm and corporate executive at Comcast, I have often been the first woman of color to assume jobs and titles. But I have never been the last. I am confident that you will be using your platform to create opportunities for people who have been marginalized, underestimated, and forgotten. I know that you are tough enough to withstand the scrutiny, the criticism, and the political winds. Be assured that you have a legion of Sisters like me who are praying for you and standing with you as you make History/Herstory again! Good Luck! Be Well! Be Safe!

Much continued success and happiness,
Charisse Ranielle Lillie

Charisse Ranielle Lillie is a businesswoman, attorney, and lecturer on issues of diversity, corporate social responsibility, and corporate governance. She became the CEO of CRLCONSULTING LLC after retiring from Comcast Corporation in January of 2017.

Chapter 68

Dear Kamala,

I have watched you, admired you, and have so much respect for you. You are the epitome of a strong black women—smart, graceful and filled with grit. I'm counting on you to becoming a bigger advocate for equality for minorities and women. I will support you and wish you an overabundance of success.

You give our young black and women of color so much to hope for, that they too can become anything they want, even the Vice President of the United States. I supported you and worked my heart out helping people to get out and vote to make help make History, HERstory.

Biden-Harris 2020. Onward and Upward!

Marnetta Malcolm

Marnetta Malcolm lives in Buffalo, New York.

Chapter 69

Dear Vice-President Harris:

Thank you for running and lending your voice for everyone in the world. I know running a campaign was not easy while balancing family obligations as well. You have inspired me to continue to be a voice for my community even when the community does not embrace you. My hope is that you continue to inspire black women from all 50 states to get into local, state, and federal positions so we can get the necessary changes we need in our communities.

I have been running for office since 2013, because I was inspired by President Obama. When I have a tough day, I rely on some quotes that remind me that I must not give in to the negativity that can come your way. I hope this brings light to any of your darkest days ahead. Human progress is neither automatic nor inevitable . . . Every step toward the goal of justice requires sacrifice, suffering, and struggle, tireless exertions and passionate concern of dedicated individuals. Martin Luther King Jr. said, "There is nothing better than adversity. Every defeat, every heartbreak, every loss, contains its own seed, its own lesson on how to improve your performance next time."

Again, thank you so much and I cannot wait to work with you to bring the change we need locally and across the 50 states.

Inspirationally Yours,
Tamika Mapp

Tamika Mapp is a mother, small business owner, Girl Scout leader, and State Committeewoman for Assembly District 68 in New York. She loves the color purple, family, and her community.

Chapter 70

Dear Vice President,

"2020." In the field of optometry 20/20 represents "perfect" vision. How ironic the original sin of America has yet again been exposed, "seen" because of the Covid-19 pandemic. During this dire time in our nation's history, we can "Restore the Soul of America"!! It is time for the spiritual reckoning and healing that is long overdue. The time has come for this country to confess, forgive, and be absolved.

I too was a little girl, also of Jamaican descent, during the Civil Rights movement and benefited from affirmative action. I continue to feel the ongoing urgency of the need for change in all systems of government. Hopefully, I will live to experience "liberty and justice for all."

Let me express how extremely proud and excited I am that our next Vice President is a woman . . . a woman of color! I am confident that the Biden-Harris team will "hit the ground running" and get the job done! (You know a woman will always identify the problem, create the solution, and make it happen!). Your life's work will be, as it has been, a beacon of light for little girls and women the world over.

Allow me to speak to the Universe on your behalf. I pray for your protection, wisdom, and peace as you continue to be a champion for human and civil rights. God be with you and your family.

Sincerely,
Marilynn Barker Martin

Marilynn Barker Martin lives in Buffalo, New York.

Chapter 71

Dear Vice President Harris:

Congratulations on being elected Vice President of the United States. I am extremely proud and happy that you were in the forefront of such an important election at such an important time in history. I stand with you as an African American woman, as a Howard University Bison alumnus, as a parent of one and step parent of five, as a change-maker, educator, and social activist. I stand with you as one who has been in the trenches and knows that our people have and continue to suffer injustices on a daily basis from the remnants of "post-traumatic slave disorder," which has diminished the humanity of all in its wake. I stand with you as a resident from the Village of Harlem and one who has worked with underserved populations throughout the five boroughs of NYC for over thirty-five years.

I have utilized the arts to address social issues such as homelessness, justice reform, educational inequity, domestic violence, poverty, mental health, and drugs. I know what it is to have policies in place which help people to grow and develop as global citizens and productive members of a community and society at large. There are over 14,000 homeless school-aged children living in temporary housing in New York City in 2020. More than half of that number reside in shelters in the Bronx. Without affordable housing and comparable wages for heads of households, these children will continue to move in a cycle of homelessness and despair without hope of making their dreams come true. Without access to equal education, the young black and brown youth will not be able to even think about rising to a position such as yours.

I have seen the difference one person can make by touching a life with no hope. I know what a flicker of light can do in a child's mind and heart. I know how they can overcome any obstacle if given a fighting chance. You are the dream of our ancestors. We all are!

I stand with you Kamala! We need you to help make a difference by standing up for those 14,000 children in NYC and around the nation who just need a fighting chance. We need you to stand up for the women and men whose voices have been silenced. Our Ancestors are walking with you! Harriet, Sojourner, Mary McLoud Bethune, Fannie Lou Hamer, Ruby Dee, Shirley Chisholm, Dr. Dorothy Height, Rosa Parks, Coretta Scott King, Dr. Betty Shabazz, Stagecoach Mary, Ida B. Wells, Maya Angelou, and all those from the "middle passage" and all those ancestors of our mothers and all those whose bloodlines run through your DNA are with you! We are all with you! No matter what they say or do, close your eyes and see all of us surrounding you at each moment. As Owen Dodson wrote, "Our mouths are dry from talking, our feet are tired from walking, but we cannot, we will not, we must not stop because ours is the unfinished song!" So, sing your song, dance your dance, and poet your words Vice President Harris!

This is your time to let them know who you are and "whose" you are! May the spirit of the Almighty Divine source guide you and protect you! May the Orisa and all the forces of nature be at your beck and call! May the ancestors uphold you and whisper to you and may you always know that you know that you know. Much love, respect, and guidance!

Truthfully yours,
Rev. Rhonda Akanke' McLean-Nur

Rev. Rhonda Akanke' McLean-Nur is an Interfaith Minister, storyteller, actress, performing arts consultant, arts administrator, and Rites of Passage and Youth Development Expert. She lives in Harlem, New York.

Chapter 72

Dear Vice President Harris,

Thank you for answering the call to serve as the Vice President of the United States. I know that your road has not been easy. When you spoke about your childhood recalling the incident about busing, I too could relate. Early on, you endured many challenges in your life, a child of divorce, a child of mixed-race parents, people asking you if you are black or your race.

You prevailed and thrived; no matter the circumstances. You attended an HBCU and became totally immersed in the school's traditions and culture. On your road to success, you attended and graduated from law school. I know that achieving these goals has not been easy. You could have chosen a position on Wall Street and made millions, but your work reflected the bible verse "To whom much is given, much is required." You chose positions in public service as the Attorney General of California and as a US Senator. You understood the importance of shattering stereotypes and utilizing those positions to be an advocate for those in need.

Along the way, you never forgot about your family. I saw you bring your extended family on stage for the celebration. I am so happy that you married a man who loves you so much that he stood in the way of someone who tried to attack you on stage.

I know that you understand the attacks are just beginning and they will increase with a vengeance. Everything about you will be scrutinized from your clothes, your hair, and including how you enter or leave a room. Just know that many women, particularly women of color, are prepared to stand with you when needed; We understand both racism and sexism. Now that you have broken the glass ceiling and became the first women of color to become Vice President of the United States,

I put on my white tennis shoes in celebration because there is so much glass on the floor.

God bless you and your family and may God bless the United States of America.

Koepia L. Merrill

Koepia L. Merrill, MA, BA, is an actress, griot (storyteller), writer, and activist. She currently resides in Baltimore, Maryland.

Chapter 73

Dear Vice President Harris:

I am so proud to have witnessed our first black President and now our first black female Vice President of the most powerful country in the world, the United States of America. What joy it brings to raise two black boys and truly mean it when I tell them that they can be whatever they want to be and that they can "dream" big. As a black woman and a member of our amazing sisterhood, Alpha Kappa Alpha Sorority Inc., I wish you and our future President Biden a successful term in the White House. I pray that you both are able to make the necessary changes to bring our country together to become what we know it can be: a country founded and built on the shoulders of immigrants, a country that loves and respects all of its citizens no matter the color of their skin, and that we will be judged only by the "content of our character." I know that you and Biden are capable of bringing our country closer to where it needs to be.

Thank you for being the strong, brave, and beautiful black woman that you are and representing all women as you make your way to the White House. And I know you will continue to make us proud throughout your term as our Vice President. You are history in the making and a force to be reckoned with!

Sincerely,
Tameka Milline

Tameka Milline resides in North Brunswick, New Jersey, where she is a Police Officer. She is also a member of Alpha Kappa Alpha Sorority (AKA) Inc., the President of the New Jersey Chapter of the International Foundation of Women (IFW), and Mrs. International 2021–Miss Tourism.

Chapter 74

Dear Vice President Harris,

Let me tell you why your journey has touched me. It is because I see small parts of your story in my own, as the only girl of 4 siblings whose immigrant parents from the West Indies met and married in London then migrated to the United States to grow a loving family and build a strong foundation in New York. Kamala, my sister, you inspire me, you inspire me to do even better, to try even harder. In you we see that all dreams are possible if we never give up. Keep striving, keep pushing, let no one turn you around, No one turn "US" around.

What an honor and how far WE have come, WE, I say, instead of You, as we travel with you, Kamala. We are in your steps and you will never walk alone. Be forever fearless. This is such an amazing accomplishment of historical proportions. I witnessed history in you!

You are the embodiment of the American Story, from two parents who met here from different places across two different seas. That love generated you and from whose maternal instruction on life guided you into your life's path. That firm foundation your mother provided and your inner compass shining so bright has led you to this day!

When the road is rocky, remember you are legion, supported by Asian women, Caribbean women, Black women. When the nights grow long, know little girls in India, Jamaica, and California are energized and inspired by the efforts of their "hometown girl." When there are doubts, look past them, knowing you are supported by generations of women who faced seemingly insurmountable odds and succeeded.

My vision for America is one where Black girls and women can look at the White House with pride. How fitting that a structure built by the toil and sacrifice of our ancestors will be graced by the first African American Vice-President. This is a symbol of the progress we have made as a people and how far we still have to go and we are getting there because of your strength and resolve. When Black women rise we are all raised up as a people, and to that ascension I say, God speed sister.

The following is a family recipe of * Peas and Rice * (West Indian Dish)

INGREDIENTS

1 (14-ounce) can light coconut milk

¼ cup water

½ teaspoon ground allspice

½ teaspoon salt

Pinch of freshly ground black pepper

3 fresh thyme

1 garlic clove, crushed

1 cup bar boiled rice

1 (15-ounce) can of pigeon peas or kidney peas if preferred, rinsed and drained

Combine the first 7 ingredients (through garlic) in a medium saucepan over medium-high heat, and bring to a boil. Stir in rice; reduce the heat to low. Cover and cook 25 minutes, or until all the liquid is absorbed. Remove pan from heat; remove the thyme and discard. Gently stir in the beans. Cover and let stand 7 minutes before serving.

Thank you for the opportunity, Vice President Harris,
Michelle Mitchell

Michelle Mitchell lives in New York City and is a member of the National Congress of Black Women Metro New York, NCNW; Long Island Cross County Section.

Chapter 75

Dear Vice President Harris,

I can only imagine how hard it must have been to get where you are today. It was so inspiring for me to see you become the first woman Vice President of the United States. Seeing you as a woman Vice President, I know that you will pave the way for girls in our future. It is very inspiring that you did not wait for another woman to be the Vice President. It is inspirational that you have the courage to even try to be Vice President. With all your hard work, you became our new Vice President. In doing so you broke down barriers for other girls and women including myself to pursue their dream.

Now that you are the Vice President it would be amazing if you could get America back in the Paris Agreement for Climate Change, because this Agreement defines rules so that we can stop Climate Change. Even the tiniest step to fight Climate Change will have an impact for our country. With several tiny steps we could stop Climate Change and that would be a HUGE milestone because Climate Change has been going on since the 1830s!

Thank you for being a role model to others and especially women.

Sincerely,
Olivia

Olivia is a fifth grader and Girl Scout from California, and loves art, the color cyan, and her trampoline.

Chapter 76

Dear Vice President Kamala,

To be young, gifted, and black is an awesome combination to reach the top. You have displayed all of these and we know you will be a great Vice President! We stand beside you, surround you, and always with you because you are a Phenomenal Woman who is leading the way for generations to come for all people! The Lord will guide you always, He will satisfy your needs in a sun-scorched land. You will be like a well-watered garden, like a spring whose waters never fail. Isaiah 58:11 NIV

Love you my sister!

Mary Ruth Morrow-Kapsiak

Mary Ruth Morrow-Kapsiak, EdM, SDA, lives in Buffalo, New York, and was Chair of the Board of Education of the Buffalo Schools. She is also a member of AKA Inc.

Chapter 77

Dear Vice President Harris,

Congratulations on becoming the first woman, Black, and Asian Vice President. Thank you for representing women and girls. It gives me hope that I can be whatever I want to be when I grow up. I hope that one day I will be as successful as you. You are an amazing role model.

Now that you are the Vice President, I request that you do something about climate change, because my generation will be the ones that have to deal with all the consequences in the future. You can create policy right now to reduce carbon emission so there would be no further damage to the climate. That would provide my generation a head start to heal this world.

Only having recently moved to the United States, I am really surprised that there is still such a lack of diversity and inclusion. I have been touched by all the recent issues with Black Lives Matter and went on a march in California to support them. You have a real opportunity to introduce policy to make sure that people of all backgrounds get equal opportunity and are treated nicely. I am trusting in your leadership.

Yours Sincerely,
Saniya

Saniya is a Girl Scout from California who was born in Australia. She loves playing soccer and doing arts and crafts and loves the color blue.

Chapter 78

Dear Vice President Harris:

ONCE UPON A TIME . . . in 2020

Before America knew it . . . in the year of the Pandemic . . . FEAR BEGIN TO PREVAIL! As such . . .

laughter, happiness, victories, mortgages/savings all begin to disappear/descend . . . even employment became at-risk

slated for only a few . . . with the Right money filled dreams . . . thus . . . goals for many were minimized and placed in drawers

Gas mask, tears, machine gun fears mass murder scenes red blood spilled into homes even on the holiest of tile floors

Taken away from loved ones . . . Borders detained children taking them from parents to assigned numbered places in cages . . .

leaving many with cobblestone thoughts of racial defeat . . . of inequalities hate filled with pain and defeat

BUT . . . THE TIME HAS FINALLY ARRIVED . . . A TIME FOR major changes! . . . and as such . . . A TOUGH ATTORNEY . . .

A WOMAN introduced as our future Vice President . . . a woman of color Kamala E. Harris appeared on the News screen TV

skies lit as women muses-former heroes/leaders lit the TORCH as former political monarch Harriett Tubman led them on!

America's grief is real! For the pains of 2020 . . . CAN SEEMINGLY NO LONGER be contained!

Thus, we can't walk away.. Public Media!..Does not even allow us to look away!

Kamala E Harris and Joe Biden you appear as medicinal shots of hope.. as our veins feeding our lives ask.. Is there HOPE?

One thing is for sure . . . we can always glance up . . . to the representation of America . . . in thought..in sight..holding a lit torch

our welcoming semblance of STRENGTH . . . the "Statue of Liberty" . . .
letting us know . . . she is there . . . to show us the way!

SHE has remained lit after many turbulent storms . . . concrete tall
resilient . . . Does it indeed take a woman to hold the Torch?

SYMBOLICALLY UNWAVERING . . . just as OUR LADY OF LIBERTY
STANDS! You've been chosen to represent steadfast in your gaze
. . . we're sure you know you will represent every one who rowed
landing upon our shores

forced and many tortured . . . worn often with newborns in their arms
. . . of every ethnicity color . . . of different colorful hues.

Know . . . believe you've been Spiritually PLACED Kamala E Harris!

and as such . . . Blessings will always be by your side for you hold Justice
. . . you hold the Truths . . .

your knowledge is to lead us on . . . THE TORCH YOU'LL CARRY FOR
US,,,we also will help you carry on!

Bev Jenai Myers

Bev Jenai Myers is a poet and painter.

Chapter 79

Vice President Kamala Harris:

We are all stronger together all because of you. Remembering the quote of civil rights activist, Fannie Lou Hamer. Montgomery County, Mississippi, with a 6th grade Education; jailed, beaten all for encouraging Black People to register to vote. She was determined to make things better. We need to figure out how we are going to make things right for all People in this country. Because of your victory, Kamala Harris, Fannie Lou Hamer is rejoicing for you. You are determined to make things better. We all know that you will figure out how we are going to make things right for all people in this country.

We are standing proud with you, Vice President Kamala Harris. Please know that Fannie Lou Hamer's work and mission still lives on today: freedom and justice for all people in this country. We are all in this together.

Congratulations,
Gwendolyn Napier

Gwendolyn Napier is a storytelling artist.

Chapter 80

Dear Vice President Harris:

I, too, am an Executive. As CEO of my company, I have had to make some unpopular decisions. But they were the "right decisions." Sometimes that is what the person in charge has to do: make the right decisions. I support you because you are "me." And, I understand that your critics do not understand that sometimes you had to make unpopular decisions. That's what you had to do. However, we have a tendency not to appreciate women in Executive positions who do what they have to do. When a male executive makes unpopular decisions, he is patted on the back and told how great he is. As a woman, we are not given that freedom, but I hereby celebrate you, support you, understand you, and, most importantly pray for you. I know that you will be not only a fabulous vice president, but, if the situation presents itself, I know you will be a great President as well. And, when you are having a bad day, sit down with your beverage of choice and read this letter.

To those younger women who feel unfairly treated because "you" were doing the best you could do at your job, remember that everything is a step *toward* perfection. I don't look for perfection until I can look in the mirror and see I am perfect. Hopefully, as they age and mature, they will understand every step you took

Sincerely,
Joyce Wilson Nixon

Joyce Wilson Nixon is Executive Director and CEO of National Inner Cities Youth, a delinquency prevention program.

Chapter 81

Dear Vice President Kamala Harris:

Thank you for pushing through the glass ceiling and taking us with you. You've shown persistence in the roles you have held. You're not only stepping up because you were highly recommended, but also from your experience. You've held some "firsts" as a woman and a woman of color. You've been tried by fire. Thank you for showing young girls that "book smart" is essential to success. You are a prime example of being young and gifted. We look forward to your future placement as Vice President of the United States of America.

You have served and showed true leadership in the various offices you have held. You've invested your time and studies and have an immeasurable amount of experience and influence to handle and succeed at this next level. We're rooting for you all the way. You're in my prayers.

Sincerely,
Nicole O'Connor

Nicole O'Connor lives in Bedford Stuyvesant, Brooklyn, and works for a government agency. In her spare time she does various works within the performance arts discipline.

Chapter 82

Dear Kamala Harris:

I don't know you personally, I only feel like I do. Actually, I only know about you. But what I have learned about you has revealed a thoughtful, courageous, determined, and committed spirit, leaving me no doubt that you are the right person to help fight for our country and save us from further irreversible destruction and devastation.

The little girl in California who you describe so poignantly, may not have been aware of the major challenges in store for her, but riding the school bus to help integrate the California public schools was just the beginning of a lifetime of preparing for those very challenges.

I, along with your throngs of supporters, know without question that you are ready for this moment. Just as you are stepping up for us—we are stepping up for you. We have your back.

With commitment and hope.

Karen Odom

Karen Odom is a writer who lives in Dobbs Ferry, New York.

Chapter 83

Dear Vice President Harris:

I'm angry.

I'm sad.

I'm in disbelief.

I don't want to believe my eyes and ears as I watch and learn as the days unfold.

I thought I knew what I believed. I thought I knew what "they" have wrong. But, then, suddenly I don't know which way is up. People I know, from colleagues to family members, are siding with what seems to be the wrong side of history. I thought I knew them. I thought we agreed, at least, on decency. I don't know anymore. Is it me that is wrong? I'm watching all sides of the news to try and see the full picture. It's hard doing all of this work in an attempt to find the unbiased facts in a sea of biases.

But. I'm also very hopeful. The day you accepted the Vice-Presidential nomination, I posted this on Instagram:#thisisnotapoliticalpost

I did not expect to be so moved this evening. As an Indian/Filipina American, a child of immigrants, married to a white American man . . . watching an Indian/Jamaican American, another child of immigrants married to a white American man, on that stage, for the first time in history . . . I realized how much representation does truly matter. If you've never been represented in the greater society, it's shocking how emotional you become when suddenly you see yourself for the first time reflected back at you. I now realize how I've acclimated and wedged myself into everyone else's American-majority reality my entire life, 47 years, simply because that's all any of us has ever known. It seems silly to say, but you can't know what you don't know, until you do. #imnotcryingyourecrying #brownskingirls.

Thank you, Kamala, for the path you have been clearing for all those walking alongside you and for those to follow. I am hopeful. I am fired up. And I am proud to be an American as you lean deeper into your leadership and embrace every individual of this incredible country of opportunity.

Sincerely,
Nina Parikh

Nina Parikh is a resident of Mississippi and shares a home with her husband, 11-year old son, a cat, and 3 fish tanks. She works in government serving the film and TV industry, teaches at Millsaps College, and volunteers with the Mississippi Book Festival, TEDxJackson, Creative Mississippi and her local chapter of the League of Women Voters in Jackson, Mississippi.

Chapter 84

Dear Vice President Kamala Harris,

I write to congratulate you on your historic success and ask you to always remember the importance of Historic Black Colleges and Universities (HBCUs). I share a part of my story because I believe you understand the need to stabilize these legacy institutions.

My memories are etched in my heart and mind. It was a hot August, Sunday afternoon when Mom and Dad drove me from the small city of Greensboro, NC, to the big city of Charlotte where I would begin my new life experience as a freshman at Johnson C. Smith University.

We arrived and saw several cars and families unloading cars on the front lawn of the dorm. My dorm was one of the newest dorms, but right away I knew it was not home. I reached deep and put on a big girl face to prevent the tears because I could not let Mom or Dad see my concern. They expected success. I was taking a step for the three of us because Mom and Dad had not attended college.

Attending college especially a Historic Black Colleges (HBCU) was a major part of the Jackson family teachings and expectations. Dad, a child of a sharecropper, had 12 siblings and worked with his three brothers to help send his sisters to college. They had all set a foundation about the importance of education to lift a family out of poverty.

I am sure many families have similar stories about their college arrivals; however, what I did not realize is that my HBCU education and experiences would shape my life forever. One cherished memory was the first day I met my best friend during a walk to the university church for Freshman orientation. I will never forget the lonely steps and the sadness I felt until I looked up and saw another girl walking alone. She smiled and introduced herself and that was the beginning of a longer conversation and laughs. We share not only our college experiences at

JCSU but also our Delta Sigma Theta pledging experiences. I am proud to say we did not let our ancestors down.

Kamala, your intelligence, and strength resonate boldly. As a graduate of a HBCU I understand that confidence and persistence. There are many graduates of Historic Black Colleges who credit their confidence and Black pride to their HBCU experiences. My choice was Johnson C. Smith University and my lifelong dedication to uplifting and empowering African Americans and serving community was cultivated as a student at Johnson C. Smith University.

I often recall with a smile sitting among my roommates and friends as we shared our dreams of career success. We will never believe anything but that our education was the best. An education that included support from family, faculty, and friends, who often told you that you could achieve and that you mattered.

The lessons were tough. As you know, high expectations and excellence were part of the success formula. So, we forged ahead to not only create a path for our career success but also for the next generation.

I would love to see a new plan for HSBCs as we prepare for a new America. Maybe now the need for quality HBCUs go beyond African Americans but become places where diamonds in the rough can shine from an array of minority groups and people born in low-income communities. The possibilities are endless. We must come together as an alumni group and reimagine the future of these historic institutions.

These colleges and universities were there for former slaves and first generations out of slavery; many coming from farm communities but now the need to uplift comes from our forgotten urban communities. The history and commitment to greatness that we all embraced are powerful and runs deep.

During your low times never question if you are good enough. As you know, you have All you need. The memories of a HSBC experience are life changing; they help shape who we are and prepare us for the challenging road of leadership.

Thank you for elevating the quality of an HBCU education. Let's plan for the NEXT.

Jennifer J. Parker

Jennifer J. Parker, JD, is the founder of Jackson Parker Communications and the Black Capital Network. Energized by making things happen and the love of community, Jennifer has served on several community boards and has received awards and nominations recognizing her work. She is a member of Delta Sigma Theta Sorority.

Chapter 85

Dear Vice President Harris,

The privilege to be a part of those who will place their thoughts and hearts in this writing to you is a wonderful opportunity, and I do not take it lightly. I was excited to know that an African American, even more specifically, a woman, would stand behind the Presidential Candidate for the 2020 Elections as Vice President of the United States of America. You have been and remain to be a fighter of injustice and one who is not afraid to take on systemic injustices, be it in healthcare, housing markets, or within and even outside of *our* communities. As your service to this Nation has caused you to rise and be a voice for the unfortunate, those who have been forgotten, and many who cry out for help but no one hears. We believe that we will now be heard as you bring issues forgotten and dismissed, which will now be brought to the light and made available for discussion.

There are many who work hard to accomplish goals that only get them to a certain pinnacle and no further. However, you are a woman of great integrity and sincere convictions. You are one who have been proven to lead those who are looking closely and those who may be looking from afar at your work, the results of what you say and the actions which you take.

We support you, stand with you, believe in you, and when the time comes, we will cry with you. But after we cry—let us get back up and fight again. There are many, so many, who are counting on you. Let that be fuel for you to know that you are not alone—and know that you do not walk, stand, or move alone. We are with you.

Most Sincerely,
Rev. Lisa R. Pate

Rev. Lisa R. Pate is a native-born Washingtonian living in Maryland, enjoying her three adult children and two grandchildren.

Chapter 86

Dear Vice President Harris:

I was born in a small village of Nepal. Nepal and India enjoy excellent bilateral ties. I grew up in a family with limited means and attended local schools. I paid the fees required by the college while at the same time helping my family with essential needs. I was able to complete the requirements to obtain a university degree from the local community college and I became an elementary school teacher. It was not easy!

As a homemaker, teacher, and wife of a country blues musician and educator, who only earns $70 per month as a salary, and who has suffered from discriminations, economic depression, and other social issues, I still believe education for every child in the world is important. I feel connected with you, Kamala Harris. You are an inspiration to women like me who want to do something for society. When I look at what you have achieved, I am encouraged and believe that I, too, can fulfill my dreams. It is difficult in patriarchal developing countries, but we have to take steps in spite of the obstacles.

Thank you for stepping forward. You are a true leader to the world, and I believe your leadership can heal race relations, end social discrimination, and other issues that we are facing. We are encouraged by what you have already accomplished and what you are yet to achieve.

Archana Risal Pokharel

Archana Risal Pokharel lives in Nepal and is a homemaker and teacher.

Chapter 87

Dear Vice President Kamala Harris,

It is so wonderful that you became the first woman Vice President. You are such an inspiration, and I will always look up to you. You make me feel proud to be a girl. I also think it is really amazing that you have accomplished so many things. You will be in the history books!

As a fifth grader, I am worried about our planet. As the Vice President of the United States, can you please help clean the oceans and make the air cleaner? If you help with this, I will feel better about going to the beach, and I'll know the animals are safe.

I am very happy that you are from California like me! And I'm glad that you're the new Vice President. I am excited to see what you will accomplish.

Sincerely,
Emily

Emily is a fifth grader and Girl Scout from California. Her favorite color is teal, she loves her cat Bob, and she loves to travel.

Chapter 88

Dear Vice President Harris:

This poem is a "love letter" to Kamala Harris but also to all of our people, especially Black Womyn. In the midst of a pandemic and the senseless murder and relentless unjustified verdict of sheroes like Breonna Taylor, we are pushed to the edges of our pain. We are at the point where there is no other choice and rainbowz ain't enough anymore. Wars are marched across our bodies in the name of political, medical, and socioeconomic gain, and no matter where we go, we still seem to represent a permanent dual underclass, Black and Womyn. We try to find pockets of hope, sunshine, vindication, and independent sovereign freedom in non-accidental moments of life.

Senator Kamala Harris's first debate was an implicit message to all Womyn, especially Black and Brown, that we have arrived in the ring (really The Oval) for battle to the blood. There is only one kind of human being that divinely possesses ovals and a period anyway. Research calls hand gestures, neck motions, and eye-sizing used by Black Womyn, Signifyin'. I feel that Senator Harris was not just signifying, she was boldly expressing in a unified manner to the world that she/we are speaking . . . and listening is no longer a request, it is required. As a Black womyn, I was finally watching a debate where I could decipher the verbal and body language of my candidate. Senator Harris demonstrated that that is no more space for pontification and negotiation. Almost every walk of civilization knows what happens when Womyn are fed up. From our ancestral greatest grandest mothers to our daughters yet to be born, the activist word in the poem attempts to communicate one message throughout many generations, whether it's traditional *"period"* or popular culture *"periodt."* We will continue to break barriers as misbehaved, nasty, monsters of immense unapologetic, revolutionary beauty. This poem is more about the knowledge and energy synergized in the power of "period." This is a time for action now. Vote. Period.

Vote.Period(t)
i called my Mom
and she said, Vote . . . Period.
She said it feels like the 1960's again.
Deep structured racism in a planned typed organization of
bad cops and klan go hand and hand,
repeated assault of the Black Man and Womyn . . . Period.
Make your voice count period.
Be like the 1980's on this November 3
and have more bounce to the ounce,
like DJ's at skating arenas,
let's dance circles around the truth,
closing tight the middle,
protecting the future of our youth.
Period.
A communal reclamation,
a one-word nation flying stealth,
and this time we got you surrounded in a "biggly" way.
Not on this Election Day.
Let a real motion be carried in a Supreme Court of Human Rights,
where your personal is political,
Black Votes Matter,
so don't believe the hype.
Period. Vote. Periodt.
Go to the polls, ballot boxes, and post offices,
wear your masks, gloves, and social-distance yourselves away from rulers
who want monarchy instead of love-based parties.
Periodt.
Vote . . . Periodt.
Vote early and vote now.
If you don't know, you better ask somebody to show you how. Periodt!
Our Ancestors died for dis' Brotha! Periodt.
And we can no longer let anotha lie for this Election. Periodt!
Vote. Periodt.
Vote. Periodt.
When it comes to the survival of humanity,

there is no other choice,
only voice.
Periodt.
Your vote is your voice. Periodt.
Vote. Periodt.
© vonetta t. rhodes

vonetta t. rhodes is a spoken art performer. She lives in Buffalo, New York, and is a member of the Ujima Theatre Group. She is also an ardent community activist.

Chapter 89

Dear Vice President Harris:

When I first discovered that Kamala Harris was a candidate for Vice President of the US, I became fascinated probably because her name sounded familiar. Then I discovered that the reason for my excitement and fascination was that her mother is from our neighboring country Nepal, which has a similar culture to mine. I am a teacher by profession and I am proud of the beautiful country of Nepal, which is still in the process of development. Seeing Kamala Harris's courage, we became motivated not just to complain but to commit to making Nepal a better country.

I am really proud to know that a "daughter" from our part of the world has gotten the opportunity to be one of the most powerful women in the world. Here in Nepal, she has become an inspiration to us to step ahead in development as we are still in a patriarchal society. I believe in her and believe that she will be able to solve the racial and social conflicts going on by taking all the people together with her.

All the best, Kamala. I have written what I felt.

Bijaya Risal

Bijaya Risal lives in Nepal and is a school teacher.

Chapter 90

Dear Madam Vice President:

Dreams do come true or, should I say faith goes a mighty, mighty, long way. What a privilege to be alive to see a woman of color as Vice President of the United States. It is evident in your speeches that your faith in God brought you to this unforgettable place in time. Your words are heartfelt and sincere. You are gracious, beautiful, and you demonstrate what it takes to reunite our country. May God continue to be your guide. Keep hold of your strong faith and courage as you move to the White House.

Let's go Kamala, you got this! The next Vice President of the United States.

You rock.

Latisa (Lisa) Roosevelt

Latisa (Lisa) Roosevelt was raised in Buffalo, New York, and is a Registered Nurse at a state facility. She received a Bachelor of Science in Nursing from Roberts Wesleyan College, in Rochester New York.

Chapter 91

Dear Vice President Kamala Devi Harris:

First, congratulations on prevailing at the polls along with President Joseph R. Biden to win the Democratic race to lead the nation during a difficult time.

When asked to write this letter, I thought about our mutual heritage as both women of African descent and the Caribbean. Though we are both Americans, this cultural background has helped us to view ourselves from a global perspective.

And, there are similarities in our lives, especially in the pursuit of a college education and careers to prepare ourselves for leadership roles in our communities. The path you took led you to a career in the legal profession and electoral politics, while I followed one in public education.

How fortunate you are to have parents that encouraged you to pursue a pathway that required dedication and commitment to a goal with a purpose as they had both achieved in their own lives as doctors in their respective fields.

From the halls of Howard University to the highest law enforcement post as the Attorney General of California, then on to the US Senate, you have shown women there isn't any mountain too high to climb when led by a purpose.

I am writing this letter as a special request to continue your leadership role in advocating against sex trafficking. It continues to be a problem both in the United States and globally. We need to do more to protect those snared into sex trafficking, especially vulnerable children, youths, and women. You had been successful in creating policies, programs, and legislation to address sex trafficking in your career as both a district attorney and Attorney General of California. While you move forward to becoming the first female vice president of the United States, your leadership in this area is direly needed to continue protecting our most vulnerable citizens from enslavement in the criminal activity of sex trafficking.

Sincerely,
Maria Rosa

Maria Rosa was born in Isabella, Puerto Rico. She lives in Buffalo, New York, and is a School Attendance Officer in the Buffalo Public Schools.

Chapter 92

Dear Vice President Harris:

When a woman has a conviction that she is doing the work God gave her to do, there is a zeal and a courage in her soul that all the forces of the world cannot destroy.

I adore you, Kamala Harris, you've made the fight worth the while. Yet, all of it is worth fighting for. You showed the world that it could be done by and for a woman. I'm ecstatic that you're bold, brave, and that you don't back down under pressure. I'm proud of you because not once did you give up and throw in the towel. I am aware that it has not been easy, believe me. I'm a Black women and I know the real struggle as I too have walked the halls of city councils and state legislators and the halls of Congress in the "poor people's campaign" fighting for our rights. We fight to live. We fight so that all of us women live. I know the set ups, the backups, and the let downs. Hear me, but you have continued to go forward in spite of it all you've endured. I commend you for your strength, tenacity and your courage. We need more women like you standing up and in the political arena. There were no stairs built for you to climb. There was no road map.

These are all signs of new beginnings. The invisible wind is strong it's lifting your wings so you can soar, flutter, and fly across the land. Forgetting yesterdays with its woes and cries—it is gone forever. Still, sad memories still linger in our minds. In these times of unrest we demand that we have women "built" into our system. They need to be women who are interested in our lives and supportive in the betterment of humanity.

At last, a woman Vice President is a first for us all. I knew it was coming, but I didn't know when. The time has finally arrived. It's been many years of hard work for us Black women. We've earned our freedom a billion times over and our convictions and perseverance held us together. We have been mocked and we have been scorned, need I say more. Please keep us beneath your wings.

Sincerely,
Shirley J. Sarmiento

Shirley J. Sarmiento lives in Buffalo, New York, and is a poet.

Chapter 93

Dear Vice President Harris:

This letter comes to you, Vice President Kamala Harris, from one of the hundreds of thousands of women on this earth—women you will never meet, shake hands with, or hear from in person—who think the world of you and are cheering you on. You have already demonstrated that you are brave enough to stand up for those of us who have never fully shared in the American dream. You've shown us through your own endeavors that it can be done, and that you are prepared to endure unimaginably offensive personal attacks to get us there.

And those attacks, untruths, and dog whistles have come directly from the President and Vice President, during and after your first publicly televised debate. They arrogantly mocked you and introduced you to a nation of voters who were selecting leaders in the most important election of their lives, using the ugliest racist, sexist epithets in the American language.

I watched in awe as you began to speak during the Vice-Presidential debate, feeling how scary that must have been for you, praying for you, and watching you come through with flying colors. No amount of interruptions, lies, mansplaining, gaslighting, or dismissiveness deterred you! As you summoned superwoman skills to stay focused, honest, rational, pleasant, and direct, while always keeping to the high road, I realized you were speaking for me, and for millions of women! From that moment on, I began to feel a connection with you that I have never felt for any political candidate before you.

I am here for you, American sister and Shero, Kamala Harris. Like countless women whose dreams you are advancing, I am used to name calling and hidden obstacles whenever I have tried to expand my personal or professional life beyond the traditional, prescribed roles for American women. From now on, I hope that you will just ignore everything ugly or limiting that is said about you. None of it is true of you—or any woman. You have everything it takes to make positive change in America, and I, along with innumerable others whose dreams you carry, stand behind and beside you. We're not giving up until we see you soar.

Sincerely,
Victoria Sandwick Schmitt

Victoria Sandwick Schmitt is an Independent Public Historian & Consultant with a special interest in women and African Americans and she lives in Rochester, New York.

Chapter 94

Dear Vice President Harris,

When one takes an X-ray, You Hold Your Breath. Your eyes and ears become the guardians of attention to all around you when you hold your breath.

In 1955, my cousin Emmett Till was killed by racists in Sunflower County, Mississippi. Hold Your Breath. Hold Your Breath. Now Breathe.

As a young teen-age girl, I was playing in a teen-age baseball tournament in Chicago's north side. The white crowd became angry because we were winning—they rioted. I ran for help—but something inside me made me stop—and I turned as the white baseball team caught up to me. I had an absence of fear—and I said, "This is wrong," they were kids too—and felt the same way. We returned to the field together to find police and an unruly, racist mob. Hold Your Breath. Hold Your Breath. Now Breathe.

As an 11-year old—I got lost on a bus—and wound up in the white suburbs of Chicago. A beefy, white policeman pulled up in his car, and he said "Hey little girlie—ya lost?" I said "Yes." He told me to get into his car and he'd take me to the correct bus. I did. He looked at me and leered, saying "Hey little girlie—how ya doing?" and patted my leg. I moved towards the door, put my hand on the handle and made up my mind to jump out of the moving car if he touched me again. He noticed—and leered broadly, saying "Hey little girlie—I ain't gonna hurt cha—ha ha ha!" Then, he drove me to my bus. Hold Your Breath. Hold Your Breath. Now Breathe.

Yolanda King (Yoli), Dr. Martin Luther King Jr.'s daughter, and I were performers at the Dallas Black Repertory Company. We were on an elevator in the hotel, after rehearsals, and Yoli missed her stop. There were two white men on the elevator with us. They said, "Well, all you have to do is jump out of the 22nd floor window to get there" and laughed. As we got off the elevator I thought—Of all the people these racists ran into, Yoli and I would straighten our backs and keep strong, Steppin' in spite of them. Hold Your Breath. Hold Your Breath. Now Breathe.

A few months ago, I was shopping in a grocery store. A young black man of 19 or 20, came up to the counter. I moved my large pocketbook. He exploded in anger and frustration, and said, "Oh, you're black like me and you're moving your purse just like white people!" My heartbeat quickened, as though it was going to crash. I looked at him and said "No, I'm moving my purse to give you some room." Tears sprang into his eyes. Then I said, "I know what you go through daily and I feel the deepness of your pain, and share your anger, and I would never do anything to hurt you." All the while, I kept gently touching his arm and he calmed down and left the store. Hold Your Breath. Hold Your Breath. Now Breathe.

Vice President Harris, these traumatic experiences did not put hatred in my heart for hatred is a mind and spirit killer. I, and countless others stand as Your Rock—Your Boulder—and together with strong people everywhere, we are your towering, majestic mountain!

Hold Your Breath. Hold Your Breath. Now Breathe.

Peace,
Dr. Glory Van Scott

Dr. Glory Van Scott is an educator, actress, and dancer.

Chapter 95

Dear Vice President Harris,

I have looked up to you with all my heart ever since you ran for President. I truly believe everything you say and love every word. I want to talk to you and be like you. I am so amazed by you and I think you are so caring. I know you will help run the country successfully.

I am glad that a woman of color was elected and a woman from Indian descent. It means a lot that we elected an Indian woman because my family is from India. Also, it makes me happy that you are from California. I hope you can help undo the wrongdoings in our country and make it the great country it was.

My whole life I've waited for a sign that we women can do big things like become the President or even the Vice President of the USA. I thought it might happen when Hillary Clinton tried, but it did not happen. Then you came along and ran for president and I thought maybe there was a sliver of hope, but I was let down again. Soon after, Joe Biden said you might be his Vice President. I was so excited. I was ecstatic on November 7, when my dad burst into our kitchen and said, "We have big news . . . the President of the USA will now be . . . Joe Biden, and his VP Kamala Harris!"

Now you are going to be Vice President, and it shows that women can continue to do great things. I wish I could meet you in person, but this letter to you will have to do. You are my role model. Thank you for all you have done for this country and thank you for what good things you will do in the future.

Sincerely,
Sonia

Sonia is a fifth grader and Girl Scout from California, and loves reading, writing, the color pink, and playing with her Malt-Tzu, Micro.

Chapter 96

Dear Vice President Harris,

A myriad of thoughts flooded my mind when I was asked to write this letter to you. Should my message be inspirational, encouraging, understanding, and supportive? I said yes to all of those things . . . What came easy was extending my sincere and heartfelt congratulations for your phenomenal and precedent setting accomplishment.

After much thought, I chose to share with you a few things that have most impacted my personal and professional lives as well as my perspective on America, as an African American woman. First, was John F. Kennedy's famous words, "ask not what your country can do for you, ask what you can do for your country." This was his call to action for each American to do what is right for the greater good. This was a noble, worthy, and aspirational goal, spoken by a privileged, wealthy white male. I will not presume to speak for all African Americans but only for myself when I say that I wait and look forward to the time when human rights and economic and justice reforms will allow all Americans, specifically African Americans, to embrace that goal and fulfill its intent. I look forward to the time when the "greater good" includes African Americans. I wait for leadership in the White House that will not contribute to the further erosion of the progress African Americans have made in seeking equality.

Sincerely and respectfully,
Joan L. Simmons

Joan L. Simmons is a Human Rights Activist in Buffalo, New York.

Chapter 97

Madame Vice President Kamala Harris:

Born and raised in my town, one had to be tough, thought-provoking, focused, and resilient to escape mindsets that believed we had to "look out for only ourselves." In order to help change mindsets that carried "dog eat dog" and "every man for himself" attitudes and ideologies, one had to rise above negativity; even in one's own family unit. No matter where negative energy came from, the challenge of removing oneself from that state is real. Perhaps the escape is mentally? Not always can we remove ourselves demographically. However, our mind can take us to places that no one can see. Education can take us places that we may not be aware of until we arrive. It shows great leadership to do what it takes to move to the next level in life. We are all human and there are times when all we have is our "God within voice" guiding us in the right direction. If we listen, in silence we can hear Him. I believe that our Creator, Father God, has a purpose for us all.

You, my dearest Queen Sis'Tar Kamala, have been a guiding light for me. My husband, Rodney, and I have been your biggest supporters long before you spoke here in Oakland, California, at your campaign stop for the Presidential Campaign last year. We were there too, rallying you on as usual. We believed that you were the best candidate for the US President. And look at God! He aligned you, prepped and molded you to be where you are today. You are meant to be our first African American Female/Woman/Queen Madame Vice President, for now. I still see you as our first African American Female/Woman/Queen Madame President. I know, one step at a time. This is your time and I hope you shine on.

I am grateful to you for hanging in there. You are so eloquent, authentic, classy, and beautiful. I know that you and your relentless tenacity will lift us from the bowels of evil. Every day I see our country destroyed emotionally, mentally, spiritually, and physically by people who support racism and an unjust government; starting at the highest level, the "white house." I believe wholeheartedly that you and our future President Joe Biden will help the American people heal. This current administration continues to divide the people, but I am hopeful that with your help, we will come together, as we are doing with peaceful protests against everything evil and vile in our country.

Thank you so much for being the change that I/We want and need to see. Thank you for giving us hope, when things seemed hopeless. I am grateful to our future President Joe Biden for choosing you to be his running mate. It is the best decision that he could have made. You were the most experienced and the greatest candidate for Vice President. That is not to downgrade any of the other females/women/Queens that were being considered for the position. They are all brilliant at what they do. But, since there can only be one Vice President, I am happy it is you! You are a phenomenal Inspirational Queen!

My husband/King Rodney and I love and appreciate you! We know that you have made sacrifices for all of your positions that you have held. I humbly thank you for standing strong for us, the people of the United States of America. I adore you dearest Queen SisTar Kamala. You have one of the most beautiful souls on this planet! You and your beautiful family are in our daily prayers. Please continue to stay happy, healthy and safe.

Love Always,
Queen Elena Delores Jones Smith

Queen Elena Delores Jones Smith is the author of *God's Radiance*, an inspirational read and gift to humanity, which she hopes will touch souls. She lives in Oakland, California.

Chapter 98

Dear Vice President/Soror Harris:

There is a continuum among generations of Black women to pass forward a baton . . . of leadership, of care giving, of social justice action. Ours, Generation X, couched between one who dragged 20th-century civil rights into televised existence and another recording 21st-century revolutions to uphold and keep those rights, has a unique positioning. We who are the beneficiaries of social justice movements, who are still often firsts and seconds—as you are the first South Asian and second Black woman to serve as Senator in United States history—are justice conduits. We keep the mantle, then teach, model, and pass on the significance and weight to this new generation: Generation Z(eal).

I call them Generation Z(eal) as they fervently and righteously poured into the streets during this pandemic wearing masks in protest to both George Floyd and Breonna Taylor's murders by law enforcement. They indignantly (and incorrectly) insisted they "are not their ancestors" and will demand the justice that never seems to come if you are not white, male, and privileged. Yet, it is up to us to show them that they *are* us—the ones who came before them. They are of us, and, as they move forward to organize and lobby, we must help them recognize the continuum of Pauli Murray, Constance Baker Motley, Diane Nash—and you.

Now in the public eye and on a political platform, Generation Z(eal) sees you. Just as you observed Senator Carol Mosely Braun push open doors as the first Black woman elected senator, representing Illinois, young women of Generation Z(eal) watch you. They noticed you entering the presidential race just as you did Shirley Chisolm and Cynthia McKinney before you. What these young women see in you is their own place at the intersection in this country. Simultaneously, they see a Black woman, a South Asian woman, a dream child of immigrants, a sorority sister, a fellow HBCU grad. They see you as a response to questions of identity when asked: What are you? Black? Bi-racial? Othered? American? The answer is simply, yes, to all of these. Identity can exist at intersections that cross, divert, and build bridges. So, when you are seen proudly dancing to drumlines, donning Howard University sweatshirts, wearing Converse or Timberland foot wear, or making masala in the kitchen with Mindy Kaling, you offer cross-sections of individuals to join with you. After all, you are an Alpha woman of the first order of Alpha Kappa Alpha women, the first Black sorority founded in 1908. As District Attorney, later elected Attorney General, then Senator—all in the state of California—you activated our sorority motto "service to all mankind" in ways that challenged and rankled, supported and affirmed those under your watch. Yet, flawed and fully human, you never left the running; instead you embraced it by pursuing the highest office as United States President. When we all see you, we are reminded of Anna Julia Cooper, intellectual, educator, and Black women's club movement leader, who famously intoned: "Only the BLACK WOMAN can say 'when and where I enter, in the quiet, undisputed dignity of my womanhood, without violence and without suing or special patronage, then and there the whole *Negro race enters with me.*'"

. . . except so many more enter with you, Soror. The survivors of the Marjory Stoneman Douglas High School shooting in 2018 forced a new generation's conversation on gun control by spearheading "March for Our Lives" in Washington, DC, that year. Emma Gonzalez, now 20, became one of the many faces for that moment, speaking and giving silent salute to the 17 who were slain from the dais. Naomi Wadler, now 14, spoke from the same platform after leading elementary classmates, at the time, on a walk-out in support of kids who had been killed though gun violence. You have already met and touched this girl, an adopted Ethiopian child, who is now a nationally known public speaker on social justice issues. There is Aalayah Eastmond, also a survivor of the Stoneman Douglas shooting, now a college student and criminal justice major, who testified before the Senate and Judiciary Committees on gun control in 2018. These young women are still engaged in grassroots work against gun violence and for voting rights, or for gender identity and equity. Even young women who are not activists in that sense, like Naomi Osaka, are watchful. Joining public protests after the shooting of Jacob Blake and murders of George Floyd and Breonna Taylor, Osaka, aged 22, pointedly wore masks with their names during the US Open. She won the tournament but also won the gaze of the world using these masks. "Before I am an athlete, I am a Black woman," she famously said, though her ethnicity, similar to yours, is Japanese and Haitian. Like you—and the other young women mentioned—she willed the watching world to pay attention to injustice and take a stand.

The continuum is here. Generation Z(eal) already has the energy and passion for justice work. They are not waiting for our mantle. We share it to give them historical reference and strength for the continued journey. But, they are watchful of you. They look for more than your symbolic representation of "other" and woman in this 2020 presidential election. They look to see how you will support, from among the highest of political offices, all of us who meet at intersections of race, gender, class, religion, ethnicity, ability, and sexual orientation. They listen for you to address them, a jaded audience who have witnessed (on social media) legal and electoral leadership fail them. How much more will you show and tell them as Vice President of the United States? I look forward to what we will teach them—in the classroom and on Capitol Hill.

Sisterly,
Dr. Shanna L. Smith

Dr. Shanna L. Smith is Assistant Professor of English at Jackson State University. Native of Kentucky, she specializes in African American Literature and Culture and has a particular interest in "young adults and social action."

Chapter 99

Dear Vice President Harris,

May I call you Kamala? Can I be candid for a moment to tell what you as Vice President means to someone like me—a millennial Black woman in America with moderate views? I see a lot of myself in you and the potentiality of what could be. You didn't follow the traditional path of what's expected of a woman—marry in her twenties with a picket fence and 2.5 kids by her mid-thirties. You are my breath of fresh air that it's okay to prioritize life on your own terms and not what society expects of you.

Black women have become the most educated and entrepreneurial group in this country. Against all odds, we've found a way to defend ourselves from all stereotypes leveled against us—questioning our integrity, our dress, our loyalty, and even our blackness. When others give 75% we are expected to give 110% and watch as other people take credit for ideas and accomplishments and never get the acknowledgement we deserve, on top of making less on the dollar than our counterparts.

To see you, a black woman, push through every hurdle put in your way—to watch you level up to the "good ole' boys club" in your career is not because of any other reason than your will power and audacity to believe that by speaking up, and not lowering your voice to a whisper, that you could change history. We see what they do to outspoken women—call us names and attempt to "put us in our place." But you never let them! You put them in their place as you eloquently trace and retrace the actions and statements of those in power who have continued to abuse their authority and whiteness to oppress people of color.

Because of you I have the audacity to dream that one day in my lifetime we will have a black woman who understands the human condition and the nuances of culture and race and sex that will unite this country against bigotry and hatred and oppression once and for all. In the midst of a pandemic, a "brewing civil war," and countless loss of lives and violations of civil liberties, we will look to you to carry and uphold the flame of justice and no one else. You will inform the future President Biden on the change that this country so desperately needs. You are the voice of the people—and will always be "Kamala for the people."

Continue to lead with empathy, grace, and confidence! We will have your back every step of the way to Pennsylvania Avenue. We will fight alongside you as you lay bare a reckoning on this country and begin the great work you were destined to do.

Love and light,
Joy Southers

Joy Southers is a Producer and lives in Washington, DC.

Chapter 100

Dear Vice President Harris:

First, I want you to know that each day I ask God to keep you safe in these difficult times. I ask that he guide you through these not so nice historic times. And, yes, they are truly historic. We have an African American woman who was elected to the second-highest office in the world. I wanted to add my name to the record of African Americans who understand how important it is to have an elected official who "looks like me," who understands my needs. I know that your mother is Indian from India and your father is a Jamaican man, but I claim you because you identify as African American and that is fine with me.

Let me tell you about my needs. I am a 78-year-old African American woman who has served my community as a child care provider. I cared for children from six weeks of age to 13 years of age. I was lucky that I never lost a child! I cared for them sick or well so that their mothers could work and support their families.

I want you to remember that child care must become a valued concern of your administration because most of the child care providers are women without Social Security, Medicare, and other means to help them live and stay strong. These care givers are also grandmothers 70–80 years of age, caring for children under the age of six. They are most vulnerable and are struggling to care for themselves as well.

Do not forget about us because we also count! And, you can count on us to support you. I am asking God to smile on you to and protect you and your family. Thanks so much for your service to this country. God Bless you and your family.

Sincerely,
Audrey Spencer

Audrey Spencer is a community quilt maker and the mother of three girls with five grandchildren and lives in Baltimore, Maryland. She is a retired child care provider, teaching assistant, and school crossing guide, and she continues to work with children in her church.

Chapter 101

Dear Vice President Kamala Harris:

I am beyond excited that your ticket won and you are now Vice President Harris! I was out of town, in the middle of rural Trump territory supporting New York with no "wifi" during the Democratic National Convention; but happily I "hot-spotted" my phone to catch the Democratic National Committee.

Black women in general have long been denied their places at the table. We have been called aggressive instead of driven, radical instead of educated, argumentative instead of articulate . . . the list can go on and on. When I saw you in the Democratic presidential debates and accepting your nomination at the DNC, I felt empowered. I felt rejuvenated. My soul sighed.

You see, I gave birth to my son three years ago in 2017. As he gestated in my womb, I thought to myself: Trump won't be president when my son reaches his teenage years. I thought that there had to be hope. Someone would come along and undo the blatant persecution of black boys, men, and women. I had to hope because I was about to become the mother of a black boy. I was already the mother of a black girl, and she was born while President Obama was in office. When she was born, I wasn't as worried about her future. I was not as worried about the heightened danger her skin tone created. I was hopeful because the President was black, his wife and daughters were black, and the President cared!

That was not the feeling I had as my son grew in my womb. It is not the feeling I have now as I watch my husband leave for work or think about my brother as he too goes to work. New York City is supposedly progressive, but things happen. My brother and husband are large black men. Both are educated and articulate. Both have loving wives and children. Both have rich brown skin. And I worry about both because of their skin. I worry that they are being judged and found dangerous just by being in existence. I worry that simple interactions can blossom into something else, something vile and dangerous and life threatening. I worry.

I worry about the millions of Americans who think racism is fabricated. The millions of Americans who do not blink an eye when another black person is killed. I worry about the millions of Americans who value the life of white people over the lives of everyone else. I worry about the millions of Americans who think property damage is justification for the use of armed force. I worry so much about the direction of this country that, as I said before, my soul hurts. I am emotionally drained by all of the televised deaths of black people. Emotionally drained about the circular conversations justifying those deaths. Emotionally drained by the continued divide: us versus them.

My soul sighed when you accepted the nomination and made that brilliant speech because I felt renewed hope. And your speech after the election was even greater. Your prior careers have given you the ability to argue both sides of the coin. Your journey, including being bused to school, shows that you know what it is like to be the unwanted black person. Thank you for stepping up. Thank you for giving me hope.

I am writing this letter because of what I envision for the United States is a tall order but I am sure you can plant the seeds that will bear fruit. I would like to see universal healthcare. Most people do not realize they need healthcare until it is too late. I would like to see health insurance companies heavily regulated and held accountable for billing. I would like to see hospitals and other medical facilities heavily regulated and held accountable for their billing. I would like universal college and graduate school. It makes absolutely no sense that one has to pay hundreds of thousands of dollars to work in a five-figure job upon graduation. I would like to see our national debt decrease and our reliance on loans from other countries cut. I would like to see the overhaul of our immigration system so that it allows for more pathways to citizenship. I would like to see published reports of border patrol stops so that we can see who is being denied entry into this county and why.

I would like to see the end of privatization of jails and prisons. I am calling for published numerical data showing those convicted on the federal level of crimes with breakdowns for crime(s), race, education, gender, assistance of counsel, appeals filed, date of incarceration, and physical location of the incarcerated person. State and federal databases with decisions broken down by judges showing their entire judicial decision history including appeals and any misconduct records. State and federal databases showing investigations and misconduct for state and federal attorneys. State and federal databases showing misconduct, riots, reports of abuse in jails and prisons. I would like to see a reemphasis on the use of clean energy and on clean water. There should be enhanced rights for the indigenous population including the right to education, medication, work, usable and sustainable land, and enhanced rights concerning their progeny. I urge updated investment plans for social security benefits insuring that all those who pay into social security will receive their benefits. The ability of those receiving social security to elect ways of increasing their benefits through the use of portals for investment (i.e., brokerage accounts.)

I want to see increased funding and plans for infrastructure. The country needs an updated nationwide railway service and dedicated roads for trucks and other large commercial vehicles. There should be updated commercial and private fly charts included in updated control towers, airports, and hangers. There should be increased safety protocols at borders specific to imports and exports. There should be refunding of the EPA with divisions working with each state on ecosystem matters.

I want to see increased funding for viral research and increased funding for genetic diseases. There should be increased funding for cancer research and increased eligibility for federal home buying grants and lower interest rates. There should be more regulation of the banking/credit card industry including penalties for redlining, predatory lending, and general banking practices (late fees, closing of accounts, over draft fees, etc.)

There should be an update of all federally installed water and water filtration systems, as well as an independent review board to test and inspect state water systems. There should be more Federal programs geared towards eliminating poverty. There should be increased trade with Canada, Mexico, South and Central America. There should be an increase in federal minimum wage levels and increased hourly wages for tip workers. There should be a decrease in the use of our military forces in foreign countries and increased funding for space exploration. And, increased funding for the security of the United States (i.e., bioterrorism/ecoterrorism detectors, missile detectors, increased sonar and satellite sweeps, etc.). There should be increased taxes on the wealthy and on businesses and decreased taxes on small businesses. There should be a closure of tax loopholes in the tax code allowing for the very wealthy to pay less taxes than the impoverished.

It is my sincere wish that your presence in office and prior to going into office continues to inspire women of color to push through walls and move mountains. It is my hope that the Black Lives Matter movement continues to be known as a civil rights movement and not linked to domestic terrorism as some have falsely represented it to be. It is my desire that calls for defunding the police be explained so that people understand it is a call for more social services outside of the purview of the police. It is my biggest prayer that my son and daughter can be safe in this country and that when they are not, the people who have jeopardized their safety are held accountable. I hope that one day this nation is ready for a black female president.

Thank you very much for reading my letter.

Sincerely,
Takara Strong

Takara Strong is an attorney, Girl Scout parent volunteer, avid reader, and lives in New York City.

Chapter 102

Dear Vice President Harris,

It was with sincere satisfaction that we heard, in France, of your nomination as Vice Presidential candidate for the American Democratic Party, alongside the future president Joe Biden. Please, accept my congratulations for being elected Vice President. It gives all women, worldwide, a sense of pride. We followed the American presidential campaign with great attention, and we had prayed that Joe Biden and yourself would win.

You are an example for all the women in this world, and you remind us that even though we are discriminated against, we can make it.

Good luck,
Alice Taha-Noel

Alice Taha-Noel is a Chef in Paris, France. She has been working at the Royal Monceau Hotel and is currently working for the Arpege company, a branch of the Elior Society.

Chapter 103

Dear Vice President Harris,

I'm super excited that we now have a woman Vice President! I think that you are going to be a great one too. I really loved watching your Vice President elect speech. What is your favorite color if you have one?

When you were a kid, what did you dream of becoming? When I grow up I want to be a doctor because I love helping people, and I'm interested in the human body. I really hope that you and President Biden help make more affordable health care for everybody. I'm originally from Canada where everybody has free health care from the government. It's not fair that some people don't get the same health care as people with money do.

Thank you so much for inspiring me in every way. I feel like I can accomplish anything now without gender bias.

Sincerely,
Ella

Ella is a fifth grader and a Girl Scout from California. She loves soccer, baking, and art.

Chapter 104

Dear Vice President Kamala,

Being the mother of two biracial children (they're grown now), I identify with your mother and understand your journey. I see in you what I instilled in my kids: strength, to stand against obstacles and bullies who try to keep them from achieving their goals. Love, for family and for themselves (that was important). I wanted them to know their family loved them and believe that they are worthy of that love. Smarts, not only book smart but people smart (Get to know people, and having people around you who are smarter then you—that way they were always learning). Faith and love of God, the most important. It's what sustained me as their mother to marry a white man back in 1979 and give them life. I know this fundamental teaching sustains them today.

Kamala, remember these teachings and all the ones your mother taught you. Start and end each day giving God thanks. You were created for His glory and to help his people. Then remember you are worthy: God says so.

Brenda Titus

Brenda Titus lives in Jacksonville, Florida, and is a retired business manager and retired restaurant owner.

Chapter 105

Thank you, Vice President Kamala Harris:

As a black woman and a mother of three daughters and one son, I'm so proud to hold you up as an example of someone who does not let anything or anyone get in the way of their dreams and their goals. You are an example of no limitations.

My children are biracial and I'm sure as you have, they also have had identity issues. It's so healthy for them and for me to have somebody they can look up to that's an upstanding woman who has confidence in herself. The way you live your life and the way you stand up for goodness and for just causes makes me want to be a better person and a better woman. I want to go back to school and pursue a higher degree and possibly, God willing, I will get a PhD.

I love that you are so smart and so beautiful, and you don't let anybody take away from the woman that your mom and your dad created and bought into this world. It makes me so proud to see somebody that's so happy with themselves and to see them achieve so much. I was so disappointed you wouldn't be the next president but I will be so excited for you to be our next vice president. Thank you for helping me be a better woman and helping me give confidence and pride to my children.

Sincerely,
Michelle Travis-Mrowzinski

Michelle Travis-Mrowzinski lives with her husband and two of her daughters in Middle Island, New York, an enclave of New York City on Long Island.

Chapter 106

Dear Vice President Harris,

Congratulations! I am so excited that you will be our next Vice President! I am happy that a Black woman will be Vice President and maybe in the future, the President of the United States! You are opening doors for me and many of my friends.

A big concern for me is climate change. It is bad for us and many different types of animals. Some ways to prevent it from getting worse might be to use more electric cars so there is not as much gas and oil being used on cars. Also, we can use less plastic and replace it with compostable materials that will not stay on the earth for thousands of years before finally breaking down.

Climate change is also impacting animals. I think that we should protect more animals and their habitats. For example, many animals are losing their homes because of people cutting down their forests. Also, in Girl Scouts we looked at the impact of plastic straws. They are getting stuck in sea turtles' noses and making it hard for them to breathe.

Plastic and other man-made objects disrupt the food chain for animals. Let's say a human puts out a poison trap because they have mice. A mouse eats a poison bait and dies. A cat finds the dead mouse and eats it. Then a few weeks later that cat gets sick and dies too and a vulture then eats it. But the vulture gets sick too because of the poison in the trap that the mouse had eaten. I think it is important to have laws that protect animals and their habitats.

Thank you for trying to make this country a better place. I hope that you and President Biden bring people together again so that there will be peace in this country.

Sincerely,
Katherine

Katherine is a creative fifth grader and Girl Scout from California, and loves dogs, soccer, and her two guinea pigs.

Chapter 107

Madame Vice President Kamala Harris,

Congratulations on adding another historical accomplishment to your record. Shirley Chisholm, Geraldine Ferraro, and Hillary Clinton all put significant cracks in the "glass ceiling" allowing you to finally break the political glass ceiling! Thank you for your example of strength, poise, and grace. Your strong-willed spirit is a model for women who are often told they are too harsh and ambitious and who refuse to stay within the societal norms of what a lady should be and how a lady should act.

As I watched you walk out to Mary J. Blige playing wearing the suffragette color, the color of the women's movement toward equality, I wanted to cry, scream, and dance. You are now representing us on the global platform and unapologetically proclaim, "Excuse me, I am speaking." You are now speaking from the position of second in command of the United States of America, and I look forward to seeing the role you will play healing and uniting our country. I look forward to seeing our youth of color puff their chest with pride, knowing every time they see you, they are seen, visible and represented on the global platform.

As quickly as possible, I need you to move beyond just being a "visual." I need you to help us get policies implemented and help change systemic rules and laws that disproportionately affect our people, all people of color. I recall you mentioning having little ability to effect change in relation to the disproportional amount of black men being incarcerated during your tenure as District Attorney in California. The system was so stacked, it was challenging for you to effect change, then. That was then and this is now. Now, I ask you to keep pushing to effect change by supporting and introducing policies to help eradicate those systemic and institutional systems that block the pursuit of happiness and prosperity in this nation for so many people of color.

Madam Vice President, there is so much work to be done. I am not expecting you to do it alone. I am willing to do my part and help in my local area. I just don't want us to get caught in the moment and miss this opportunity to expand upon the historical time. I don't want us to get caught in the honeymoon stage and before we know it, four years later, very little change occurs.

I ask that you consider:

- Universal Health Care for all Americans
- Pursue the most aggressive policies available to protect and preserve our planet for all future generations. I know you believe in science and so you know Climate Change is real.
- Working for the over 140 million voters who cast their votes in this election. A large percent of whom are hard-working and suffering to keep food on the table and a roof over their heads.
- Educational policies that help children in low income neighborhoods level the playing field.
- Discontinue the focus of the stock market, Wall Street, and corporate interests. Increase their taxes along with high income citizens so they are contributing their fair share.
- Do not privatize our Social Security and Medicare. To maintain equity, it must remain a federally run program.
- Eradicating suppression of voters' rights in states where evidence shows it exist. Make it easier for people to vote using ballots and secure online options.

I look forward to your continued historical path, I look forward the next four years. I look forward to the legacy you create and leave behind.

In sisterhood and love,
Simone-Monet Wahls

Simone-Monet Wahls was born in Manhattan raised in Brooklyn. Along with other selected business leaders, she was invited twice to the White House under the Obama Administration. She is Founder of Future Executives Inc. and founding Cochair of the National Congress of Black Women, Metro NY Chapter.

Chapter 108

Ms. Vice President Harris,

These times are strange. Harrowing even. As a young black, queer, female, the weight of it all seems to trap me—like in those dreams where you try to run but you barely move forwards (like you're running through quicksand) and whatever it is that's chasing you inevitably catches up . . . and you wake up (or perhaps fall asleep). These times are disheartening—but you bring with you the potential promise of something better.

I know many people my age, especially those existing within minority groups, went out to the polling booths begrudgingly. Offering support as a way out of the current situation, but not necessarily because they wanted to. Personally, I knew that I wished I could go back to worrying about things like the housing market and not if I would lose one of my trans friends or family members, or if one of my brothers would lose their life to police violence.

I know that I believe in you. And I'm so, so proud of all you've done thus far. You have our support behind you, but please, vote for us as we voted for you.

All the very best,
Katiana Weems

Katiana Weems currently resides in Baltimore, Maryland, and teaches editing and visual storytelling at Baltimore School for the Arts. She is an award-winning director, cinematographer, and editor, and her work has been screened internationally and featured in the *New York Times*.

Chapter 109

Dear Vice President Harris:

I want to tell you about THE DAY THE MUSIC STOPPED:

As a former caregiver, and daughter of a father who valiantly battled Alzheimer's disease, I humbly ask you to please join the fight to end the 6th leading cause of death in the United States. I like YOU am on a mission; my goal is to end this disease, which strips men and women of their memories and dignity. As a volunteer board member of the Alzheimer's Association of Western New York, I fight in memory of my Dad, who was a brilliant, fun-loving, kind businessman, musician, and father of 5 children, grandfather, and great-grandfather who regularly serenaded my mother with love songs until one day he put down his beloved, shiny Selmer saxophone and the music stopped.

Today I fight in every way I can for all those who cannot speak for themselves. As the number of Americans grows rapidly so too will the number of new and existing cases of Alzheimer's. Did you know that one in 10 people age 65 and older (10%) has Alzheimer's dementia? Almost two-thirds of Americans with Alzheimer's are women. Older Africans are twice as likely to have Alzheimer's or other dementias as older whites. Did you know that Hispanics are about one and one-half times as likely to have Alzheimer's or other dementias as older whites? A startling fact, more than 5 million Americans are living with Alzheimer's as you read this. By 2050 the number of people age 65 and older with Alzheimer's dementia may grow to a projected 13.8 million barring the development of medical breakthrough to prevent, slow, or cure the disease. More than 16 million Americans provide unpaid care for people with Alzheimer's or other dementias. The untold story here, Alzheimer's takes a devastating toll on caregivers, emotionally and financially. I survived by the grace of God and by a loving, supportive safety net created by family, friends, and the Alzheimer's Association and its network of partners, volunteers, and sponsors. The plight of the caregiver doesn't make headlines often but I know from personal experience this disease will one day affect someone you know or love.

It was a really hard experience for me, to witness my Daddy battle this disease. Many times, I found myself swallowing my tears as I lifted him and placed him in a Hoyer apparatus so I could move him from the living room to his bedroom. I kept things light, and we laughed about it and made jokes. I smile thinking about it. I found joy through my own personal faith to weather this storm. Kamala, I learned so much caring for him, I want to share it and valuable information and resources with others in documentaries, films, television, and podcasts so that they will be able to navigate this journey.

One day, my Daddy told me, LOVE IS THE ANSWER; he said this while resting in his easy chair, eyes closed as he listened to me— in a manic state, hair all over my head, irritated and exhausted, railing at a surprised well-meaning sibling. My sibling didn't deserve my rant and father knew it. LOVE IS THE ANSWER, he said, resting and reflecting. I guess all closed eyes aren't sleep. LOL! As researchers move closer to finding a cure, I am not sitting and waiting for it. I am laser focused, using my imagination, heart and faith to educate, empower, and inspire.

Did you know, $244 billion dollars' worth of care is given by family members and other unpaid caregivers? Who are the caregivers? About one in three (30%) is age 65 or older. Approximately two-thirds are women, and one-third are daughters. Most live with the person with dementia in the community and one-quarter are "sandwich" generation caregivers, caring for an aging parent and children under the age of 18. These facts provided by the Alzheimer's Association of America are glaring, sobering, and for many of us over 50 a little scary.

Kamala, this is what I ask: Commit to a CURE! Increase funding for research, Increase financial support for respite care, Increase financial support for caregivers, Increase public engagement and outreach to African American and Hispanic communities, and call for an Education Campaign on how health disparities impact at risk Black and Brown communities. Create a special office in the White House to focus all of these existing efforts and challenges with a strategic, comprehensive plan.

I ask you to join and support us! Do not forget us, Sister, we have not forgotten you. We Love you. If you are reading this please share this information within your broad networks.

Sincerely,
Sandy White

Sandy White is a Buffalo, New York, native, and a journalist, urban planner, filmmaker, and owner of the Mustard Seed World Consulting Group.

Chapter 110

Dear Vice President Harris,

I am so excited for you to be our next Vice President of the United States of America. I voted in person at one of our early voting locations here in Georgia; I didn't trust the mail. I am equally as excited for Joe Biden to be our next President. I am a lifelong Democrat. I am 52 years old and I vote at every election, whether local or Presidential. I don't take my right to vote for granted because I know that it took a lot of good determined people for us to gain that right. I want us to keep it. As a responsible citizen I try to vote for what's best for the least of us, not just the wealthy. I am for the people. I believe to whom much is given much is required. If I have to pay a little more for the less fortunate to have a better life with food and shelter and provisions for their family like excellent schools for their children etc., I will do that gladly.

My main concern for this election was for a complete overhaul of the criminal justice system and raising the minimum wage to fifteen dollars an hour. I believe with your background and leadership we can get some measurable changes done in four years. I know we need Congress to help you and Joe, therefore I voted blue down the ticket.

I just want you to know that I am praying for you and Joe daily. I believe in you and I believe in the American democracy. We are a melting pot and our leadership should reflect that in public offices especially. You are qualified for this job and more.

This is the time and the moment for you. Be well, be great, and be bold. Got your back! From a lil ole' country woman in Stonecrest,

Georgia, may God bless you and may God bless these United States of America!

Sincerely,
Tina White

Tina White is a 52-year old Christian, educated, southern, African American woman born and raised in Tifton, Georgia, and now working in the metro Atlanta area as a manager in the field of Accounting.

Chapter 111

Dear Soror Kamala,

Several months ago, I embarked on a journey to impact change. The journey led me to confront the persistence of systemic racism, white privilege, and white supremacy delusion at America's oldest continuously published general interest magazine, shedding light on its biased recruitment, hiring, and procurement practices that suppress opportunities for African Americans and people of color. It took the greatest willingness I have ever called upon in myself to speak my truth.

I did not shy away from giving specific details of my and others' experiences of racial bias. I firmly believe to push through general demands for change, the truth requires concrete examples, with a light shown into the crevasses. This is not easy.

I can only imagine how many moments in your life have not been easy. And yet, here we stand, with your purpose in this movement, shinning on each of us. You have made history as the first woman, and the first Black woman, to hold the second highest office in our nation. It gives me strength and motivation to press on another day.

In the end, I took my shot, and the risk of speaking up not for myself but for all those who look like me to have a different experience going forward.

Because of you, I dreamed, and I dared to tell the truth. There will be more to come.

Thank you for your fortitude, perseverance, and steadiness. You inspire me.

Sisterly,
Verneda Adele White

Verneda Adele White is a contributing writer and social entrepreneur. As the Founder and Creative Director of Human Intonation, her works spanning the fashion, philanthropic, and events industries continue to advocate for change for critical social & human rights issues, HIV/AIDS, racial justice, and climate change.

Chapter 112

Dear Vice President Harris:

First and foremost, congratulations on your nomination as the Democratic Vice-Presidential Candidate of the United States and that incredible win for the Vice Presidency! What a historic accomplishment. "Proud" does not express just how exuberant many women are to bear witness to you in this position. I truly believe that you are the change that is essential to our nation.

Throughout the years, you have advocated for public safety as a lawyer, brought justice to the forefront as the first African American female Attorney General for the State of California, and continue to serve as a United States Senator. You have been the "first" for many positions in leadership and have inspired brown and black women, both young and old, across the country. As an elected official in the City of Buffalo, New York, I understand the monumental undertaking of being the "first." All eyes are watching to see what your next move will be. There is an immense amount of pressure coming from all directions. But you have far exceeded all expectations in accepting and conquering every challenge thrown your way.

Finally, I would like to share with you a memory that calms me at the end of a long work day. The phrase "Good and Faithful Servant" comes to my mind because it is a phrase that I recall from my youth as I listened to the mothers of the church. Yes! That spiritual root is my lifeline. So, every day, if you ask yourself: 'Have I done the best that I could do?' and the answer is yes, then you, my faithful sister, have done all that needs to be done that day. We are grateful that former

Vice President, Presidential Candidate Joseph R. Biden Jr. has chosen wisely. I wish you great success as you travel the road ahead.

Sincerely,
Barbara Miller-Williams

Barbara Miller-Williams is the first African American and female Comptroller for the City of Buffalo, New York. She is a lifelong servant of the community, Retired Master Sergeant/US Army and former City of Buffalo Police Officer.

Chapter 113

Dear Vice President Harris:

Kamala Devi Harris, born in Oakland, California, to Donald Harris, a Jamaican, Stanford University Professor Emeritus of Economics. Her mother, Shyamala Gopalan was a biologist whose work on progesterone receptor gene stimulated work in breast cancer research. Her maternal grandfather's progressive views on democracy and women's rights left an indelible mark on her. Having visited both India and Jamaica, Kamala is strong because she is rooted in culture and family history. As a young girl starting school for the first time, Kamala was put on a bus every day as part of Berkeley's comprehensive desegregation program and the school landscape changed from a previously 95% white student culture to a 40% black student culture. Kamala attended an African American church in Oakland and sang in the children's choir. Her mother introduced her to Hindu mythology and she attended the Hindu temple. Her parents went through a domestic reorganization when she was 7 and at age 12, her mother moved she and her sister to Canada.

A new culture is ushered in to inform what will come next for the creature of divine guidance. The tongue tells the stories of youth. The ear listens for the stories of the elders. The heart treasures the stories of the ancestors.

In Canada, Kamala attended a French-speaking elementary school and graduated from high school in 1981. She continued her education at Howard University and graduated with a BA degree in political science and economics. She did not stop there. She went on to the University of California–Hastings and received her law degree. She received an honorary Doctor of Law degree (LLD) from the University of Southern California and an honorary Doctor of Humane Letters (DHL) from Howard University in 2017. Kamala is a proud member of the Alpha Kappa Alpha (AKA) Sorority. The life of an industrious woman is free from mischief. Kamala is a symbol of hope in the spirit of truth. Never allowing the bear to jump on her back.

Kamala is a United States Senator (D) from California; former District Attorney of San Francisco; advocate for healthcare reform, ban on assault weapons, progressive tax reform, while paving a way for undocumented immigrants. Kamala was the one who stood firm in asking pointed questions of the Trump administration officials during Senate hearings. Kamala attracted national attention when she bravely and courageously ran for the 2020 Democratic presidential nomination. She is the first African American woman, the first Asian American woman, and the third female vice presidential running mate on a "major" party ticket after Geraldine Ferraro and Sarah Palin.

All good intentions align in the corridor of mercy. Judgment must wait to hear all the witnesses. We are riven with deeply marred, cracked, and splintered places that need healing. Kamala is called to the work of mending this dilapidated, damaged country. In 2005, the National Black Prosecutors Association honored Kamala with the Thurgood Marshall Award. She was featured with 19 other women in a *Newsweek* report profiling "20 of America's Most Powerful Women." In 2006, she was elected to the National District Attorneys Association board of directors as vice president and appointed to cochair its corrections and reentry committee. In 2008, Kamala was named one of 34 attorneys of the year by *California Lawyer* magazine. A *New York Times* article published later in 2008 identified her as a woman with potential to become president of the United States, highlighting her reputation as a" tough fighter." In 2010, California's largest legal newspaper, the *Daily Journal*, designated her as one of the top 75 women litigators and one of the top 100 lawyers in the state. In 2013, *Time* named her one of the "100 most influential people in the world." In 2016, 20/20 Bipartisan Justice Center awarded her the Bipartisan Justice Award along with Senator Tim Scott. In 2018, she was named the recipient of the ECOS Environmental Award for her leadership in environmental protection. Kamala is a member of Third Baptist Church of San Francisco, a congregation of the American Baptist Churches USA.

And finally, Dearest Kamala, surround yourself with people who will have something thoughtful to say when your documentary is made.

You are called to rebuild, repair, reconcile, restore, regenerate, revive, rejuvenate, and soothe. Keep your eye on the landscape, an ear to the pulse, with a vision to nurture, lifting America to the light towards reconciliation, in the loop of justice with an investment in equity. Breathe in and out. Kamala, you were born an original, not a copy.

May the blessings of the day grab you and shake your hand.

Diane Williams

Diane Williams has been a professional storyteller in many forms for more than 25 years. As an author, performing artist, storyteller, teaching artist, speaker, consultant, and mixed-media fiber artist, she delights in crafting narrative tapestries that educate, entertain, and bring people together.

Chapter 114

My Dearest Vice President Kamala Harris:

I have lived in the Village of Harlem, the Black Mecca of America, for the majority of my adult life. I grew up in Queens, New York, and experienced the trauma of being bused from my South Jamaica middle-class Black neighborhood to the richest area in Jamaica Estates where I received a great competitive education but learned about the division of race early though it was not overt. Fast forward, I survived High School by returning to my neighborhood school, allowing me to concentrate on my education and personal development devoid of the race card until a busload of Police Officers sat outside my school and watched a white male boy stab a Black male student and did nothing until Black students retaliated. It was then I knew I could not attend a white college institution and concentrate on my education and self-development. I chose the great Alma Mata of my dear Uncle Bob—the great Lincoln University—when Gil Scott Heron was there and started his band. He was a personal friend.

At Lincoln University in 1969, we were political, we were valiant, we were powerful, we were brilliant. We were conscious and unapologetically Black. Our school year ended with a candlelight vigil for the students who were killed by Police at Kent State and Jackson State, followed by the Klan burning unmarked crosses on our Lincoln University campus, which forced us all to leave the campus with all our possessions we could carry two weeks before the semester ended. I transferred to Fordham University, one of the most racist institutions in the country, but I received extensive training in Media and graduated early with a BA in Mass Media to escape the racism and abuse. Looking back on life, staying at Lincoln would have been a better choice, but obviously my life journey has brought me to where I stand strong today.

I gave you some of my background to explain that I am a quintessential revolutionary who is unapologetically Black. My background is African, Cherokee Native American, and my great-grandfather was white, but in America I am classified as Black, and I am unapologetically Black. I have fought and experienced racial disparity my entire life. I am a graduate of the WNET Television Training School. I am a member of several media unions and have worked at all the networks. I was married twice and a single mother of two adult children and four grandchildren, the oldest who is a senior at Howard University. I was qualified, qualified and still denied much in the media world. I became a Harlem entrepreneur and homeowner—qualified, qualified and still denied even Empowerment Zone Funding designated for our community. I am a new Community Board Member here in Harlem and the Host and News Director for a new Harlem Media Platform, "Harlem Network News." I am talking and walking the walk. I have experienced American first hand, up close, personally witnessing racism and bias as a women in salary, promotions, housing, and other opportunities. Living in Harlem a majority of my adult life and raising my children, I am the child of Southern migrant grandparents who migrated to Harlem, raised their families and then moved to the suburbs of Queens and Yonkers.

I lived and have layers of Black American life and now I am known as an Elder. I love my precious Harlem with the good, the bad, and the ugly and have endured it all and seen the change as Harlem gentrified—the change in services, the change in facilities and businesses, all a benefit in many ways to the community. But why did whites have to come to get garbage picked up that all our taxes pay for? However, though Harlem is gentrified, the Public Schools in Harlem are 99.99 per cent all Black and Brown students, and they are indeed substandard. The education here in Harlem is separate but not equal. I would say 50% of our Harlem Community has family members who have at some point been incarcerated, including mine, no matter what the economic, educational background of the family—this is a global Black reality. Most of the new housing and old housing in Harlem is not affordable to a majority of the Black and Brown Community. Harlem, of all of the 62 counties in New York City, was the hardest hit by Covid-19 infection and death; and "still we rise." We are the survivors of the survivors—we are a resilient people.

At the onset of Covid-19, I along with my partner launched a new media platform, Harlem Network News, dedicated to assuring that "Harlem" and the Harlems of the world are informed—"knowledge is power." It has been quite a journey and Harlem Network News has been extremely effective interviewing Public Officials, Clergy, and Harlem Doctors as well as covering on-site Clergy Marches for Freedom, the Black Lives Matter Harlem Mural, Stop the Violence Groups, i.e., Street Corner Resources, Community Tributes to Harlem Hospital Doctors, Nurses, and Workers, as well as the March on Washington—"Get Your Knee Off Our Neck." We are growing and developing though Harlem Network News, seeking funding, grants, and support. We are resilient and our content is strong.

Vice President Kamala Harris, we truly need you and President Joe Biden to literally come to Harlem and conduct a Town Meeting from the acclaimed Apollo Theatre—of course talking to a virtually empty room—armed with your outline for what you are going to do for Harlem and the Harlems of the country to end racial, economic, housing, and medical disparities. This would show you both are proactive in your efforts for change and connection to communities of color. There must be a plan in place as to how we, the black and brown community, can submit a strategic workable plan and form a task force to work with you and President Biden.

It is my contention that we need what mirrors a "Reparations Initiative Program" that will fund our entrepreneurs and businesses, bring adequate medical care and facilities to our neighborhoods, enhance the separate but not equal education our children are receiving, and assist folks in paying their rent and paying off their children's college loans. Or, paying for their children's college education whether they attend public or private institutions. A Reparations Initiative would have to be properly managed and dispersed by an independent organization in conjunction with the government. Current funding earmarked for our communities never reaches our communities. This practice must end. Separate institutions that are equal, run properly, educating young people, and building cultural awareness and great self-esteem are needed. Your Alma Mata Howard University and my Alma Mata

Lincoln University and many of the HBCU's are prime working examples of success.

Finally, the basis of our issues is economics, and we are indeed deserving as we came as slaves, built this country as slaves on slave wage labor and "still we rise." The playing field must be systemically leveled, and we are counting on you and President Biden to begin this process, lest the country fall further into anarchy, civil unrest, and ultimately Civil War as open season for Black people being killed by the police and now vigilantes is rampant. We have suffered the Coronavirus Pandemic this year and the Pandemic of Racism for 400 plus years. This is our time, and we need you and President Joseph Biden to stand with and for us and deliver—deliverables matter! We Matter!

In Great Gratitude and Faith,
Sister Terri Wisdom

Sister Terri Wisdom lives in Harlem and is the Director of Harlem Network News.

Chapter 115

Dear Vice President Harris,

We are truly honored to be writing to a Black woman who holds so much power for her people. Congratulations on everything you have accomplished & are continuing to accomplish. We are very proud of you.

We are close friends who also have done a lot of work together as Youth Organizers at the Center for Teen Empowerment in our neighborhood and as RocResponders who run restorative circles at Wilson Commencement High School in Rochester, NY. One of us (Amarye) is also a Youth History Ambassador, working with elders who grew up on Clarissa Street where the highway and urban "renewal" (removal) ripped apart a strong African American community. We are carrying forward their legacy and teaching people in our city and suburbs about how racist policies created the inequality we see all around us, so that we can find ways to repair the harm.

Destiny wrote a poem that will tell you about how powerful we are, and how we must learn from history to show us the root causes of the issues that we as Black, Brown and mixed-race youth have to live with every day in America.

"Untitled," by Beautiful Destiny Ford

I Am an African American girl.
With broad hips, thick lips and when my hair gets wet it curls.
In most cases I'm the head of the house, and NO, I don't "talk white."
    I speak proper.
I come from greatness, my ancestors were most likely sharecroppers.
I'm educated, but not enough.
I was never taught in school how African Americans can use and
    manipulate tools the way we do. We made:
-Irons,
-Dustpans,

-Combs,

-The first traffic light,

Let me know how Thomas Edison's lightbulb would have shined if a
black man didn't create the carbon filament to go inside

-from the gas furnace, to the gas mask it was created by BLACK HANDS

Yet, we were called "porch monkeys," "ignorant". Let me know how
"ignorant porch monkeys" contributed so much to the society we
know today. . . .

I'm labeled a menace for havin' melanin. I'm tired, so tired of being
tired. I'm tired of being an outcast. I'm tired of racism putting me
last,

Making me feel like I'm less of a person because my hips are spread wide

And calling me an angry Black girl because I refuse to lie.

Well, I can't change my skin and I refuse to perm my hair just to fit
in, somewhere I'm not welcome. America

Please tell me, what did I do so wrong?

Born and raised in the U.S., but it feels like I don't belong.

Where guns are valued more than students

Where books that can actually educate are banned from schools

Where schools are constantly failing our children, and we wonder
why America is no longer winning.

Where our Black males are set up for criminal lives

Where mumbling rappers are overpaid and teachers are underpaid,
and we wonder why the graduation rates are so low.

Segregation is sugar-coated

African Americans are still slaves, we just don't know it

Where PTSD, depression and anxiety are swept under the rug for
people that look like me

Where babies raise babies and young boys are forced into men

Where police are allowed to do everything but serve and protect

Where having white skin is somehow a bullet-proof vest

Where we take one step forward and ten steps back

Back into the past

That we

Refuse

To talk about.

We refuse to *NOT* talk about the past, the present and the future we must build. Everything we do for our people and for ourselves makes us happy—speaking for the unspoken, the broken and oppressed. We and our elders show everyday how strong we are even as we are faced with the unthinkable.

We will keep learning from the past to understand today so that we can keep fighting for change in our community.

We get our peers to talk about what's going on for them and to work out their problems with each other. We can only do this when people in power stop criminalizing and suspending students. We need your help with that. We feel safest when youth in our neighborhoods have jobs and access to support systems that help our mental health, not when our streets are filled with police and violence. We need to reimagine what is real public safety, not just throw together a few police reforms.

In the middle of last school year, we had to fight budget cuts by doing student-led walkouts, speaking out in school board meetings and lobbying our "representatives" in Albany. They still took more than 100 teachers out of our schools. We need our government to end school funding that is based on unequal wealth and focus on bettering the youths' education and mental state.

We want to have the beautiful community our elders created even amidst racism and redlining. We need policies that help Black families get back what was taken from them and build up wealth like white families were able to back then.

We will keep marching forward and taking stands on what we believe in. We need you to stand up for us. You have access to power not available to us. We need you to push for change like we are.

Yours truly,
Amarye Woods and Beautiful Destiny Ford, young students
from Rochester, New York, writing together.

INDEX OF CONTRIBUTORS